J. H. Miller.

𝕽𝖎𝖛𝖊𝖗𝖘𝖎𝖉𝖊 𝕰𝖉𝖎𝖙𝖎𝖔𝖓

———◆———

CONDUCT OF LIFE

BEING VOLUME VI.

OF

EMERSON'S COMPLETE WORKS

THE

CONDUCT OF LIFE

BY

RALPH WALDO EMERSON

New and Revised Edition

BOSTON
HOUGHTON, MIFFLIN AND COMPANY
New York: 11 East Seventeenth Street
The Riverside Press, Cambridge
1886

The Riverside Press, Cambridge:
Electrotyped and Printed by H. O. Houghton & Co.

CONTENTS.

———◆———

I.

FATE.

———◆———

DELICATE omens traced in air
To the lone bard true witness bare;
Birds with auguries on their wings
Chanted undeceiving things
Him to beckon, him to warn;
Well might then the poet scorn
To learn of scribe or courier
Hints writ in vaster character;
And on his mind, at dawn of day,
Soft shadows of the evening lay.
For the prevision is allied
Unto the thing so signified;
Or say, the foresight that awaits
Is the same Genius that creates.

FATE.

IT chanced during one winter a few years ago, that our cities were bent on discussing the theory of the Age. By an odd coincidence, four or five noted men were each reading a discourse to the citizens of Boston or New York, on the Spirit of the Times. It so happened that the subject had the same prominence in some remarkable pamphlets and journals issued in London in the same season. To me however the question of the times resolved itself into a practical question of the conduct of life. How shall I live? We are incompetent to solve the times. Our geometry cannot span the huge orbits of the prevailing ideas, behold their return and reconcile their opposition. We can only obey our own polarity. 'T is fine for us to speculate and elect our course, if we must accept an irresistible dictation.

In our first steps to gain our wishes we come upon immovable limitations. We are fired with the hope to reform men. After many experiments we find that we must begin earlier, — at school. But the boys and girls are not docile; we can make nothing of them. We decide that they are not of

good stock. We must begin our reform earlier still,
— at generation : that is to say there is Fate, or
laws of the world.

But if there be irresistible dictation, this dictation understands itself. If we must accept Fate,
we are not less compelled to affirm liberty, the sig-
nificance of the individual, the grandeur of duty,
the power of character. This is true, and that
other is true. But our geometry cannot span these
extreme points and reconcile them. What to do?
By obeying each thought frankly, by harping, or, if
you will, pounding on each string, we learn at last
its power. By the same obedience to other thoughts
we learn theirs, and then comes some reasonable
hope of harmonizing them. We are sure that,
though we know not how, necessity does comport
with liberty, the individual with the world, my polarity with the spirit of the times. The riddle of
the age has for each a private solution. If one
would study his own time, it must be by this
method of taking up in turn each of the leading
topics which belong to our scheme of human life,
and by firmly stating all that is agreeable to experience on one, and doing the same justice to the op-
posing facts in the others, the true limitations will
appear. Any excess of emphasis on one part would
be corrected, and a just balance would be made.

But let us honestly state the facts. Our America has a bad name for superficialness. Great men, great nations, have not been boasters and buffoons, but perceivers of the terror of life, and have manned themselves to face it. The Spartan, embodying his religion in his country, dies before its majesty without a question. The Turk, who believes his doom is written on the iron leaf in the moment when he entered the world, rushes on the enemy's sabre with undivided will. The Turk, the Arab, the Persian, accepts the foreordained fate:

" On two days, it steads not to run from thy grave,
    The appointed, and the unappointed day ;
  On the first, neither balm nor physician can save,
    Nor thee, on the second, the Universe slay."

The Hindoo under the wheel, is as firm. Our Calvinists in the last generation had something of the same dignity. They felt that the weight of the Universe held them down to their place. What could *they* do? Wise men feel that there is something which cannot be talked or voted away, — a strap or belt which girds the world : —

"The Destiny, minister general,
  That executeth in the world o'er all,
  The purveyance which God hath seen beforne,
  So strong it is, that though the world had sworn
  The contrary of a thing by yea or nay,
  Yet sometime it shall fallen on a day
  That falleth not oft in a thousand year ;
  For, certainly, our appetités here,

Be it of war, or peace, or hate, or love,
All this is ruled by the sight above."
CHAUCER : *The Knighte's Tale.*

The Greek Tragedy expressed the same sense. " Whatever is fated, that will take place. The great immense mind of Jove is not to be transgressed."

Savages cling to a local god of one tribe or town. The broad ethics of Jesus were quickly narrowed to village theologies, which preach an election or favoritism. And now and then an amiable parson, like Jung Stilling or Robert Huntington, believes in a pistareen - Providence, which, whenever the good man wants a dinner, makes that somebody shall knock at his door and leave a half-dollar. But Nature is no sentimentalist, — does not cosset or pamper us. We must see that the world is rough and surly, and will not mind drowning a man or a woman, but swallows your ship like a grain of dust. The cold, inconsiderate of persons, tingles your blood, benumbs your feet, freezes a man like an apple. The diseases, the elements, fortune, gravity, lightning, respect no persons. The way of Providence is a little rude. The habit of snake and spider, the snap of the tiger and other leapers and bloody jumpers, the crackle of the bones of his prey in the coil of the anaconda, — these are in the system, and our habits are like theirs. You have

just dined, and however scrupulously the slaughter-
house is concealed in the graceful distance of miles,
there is complicity, expensive races, — race living
at the expense of race. The planet is liable to
shocks from comets, perturbations from planets,
rendings from earthquake and volcano, alterations
of climate, precessions of equinoxes. Rivers dry up
by opening of the forest. The sea changes its bed.
Towns and counties fall into it. At Lisbon an
earthquake killed men like flies. At Naples three
years ago ten thousand persons were crushed in a
few minutes. The scurvy at sea, the sword of the
climate in the west of Africa, at Cayenne, at Pan-
ama, at New Orleans, cut off men like a massacre.
Our western prairie shakes with fever and ague.
The cholera, the small-pox, have proved as mortal to some tribes as a frost to the crickets, which,
having filled the summer with noise, are silenced
by a fall of the temperature of one night. Without
uncovering what does not concern us, or counting
how many species of parasites hang on a bombyx, or
groping after intestinal parasites or infusory biters,
or the obscurities of alternate generation, — the
forms of the shark, the *labrus*, the jaw of the sea-
wolf paved with crushing teeth, the weapons of the
grampus, and other warriors hidden in the sea, are
hints of ferocity in the interiors of nature. Let us
not deny it up and down. Providence has a wild,

rough, incalculable road to its end, and it is of no use to try to whitewash its huge, mixed instrumentalities, or to dress up that terrific benefactor in a clean shirt and white neckcloth of a student in divinity.

Will you say, the disasters which threaten mankind are exceptional, and one need not lay his account for cataclysms every day? Aye, but what happens once may happen again, and so long as these strokes are not to be parried by us they must be feared.

But these shocks and ruins are less destructive to us than the stealthy power of other laws which act on us daily. An expense of ends to means is fate; — organization tyrannizing over character. The menagerie, or forms and powers of the spine, is a book of fate; the bill of the bird, the skull of the snake, determines tyrannically its limits. So is the scale of races, of temperaments; so is sex; so is climate; so is the reaction of talents imprisoning the vital power in certain directions. Every spirit makes its house; but afterwards the house confines the spirit.

The gross lines are legible to the dull; the cabman is phrenologist so far, he looks in your face to see if his shilling is sure. A dome of brow denotes one thing, a pot-belly another; a squint, a pug-nose, mats of hair, the pigment of the epidermis,

betray character. People seem sheathed in their
tough organization. Ask Spurzheim, ask the doctors, ask Quetelet if temperaments decide nothing?
— or if there be anything they do not decide?
Read the description in medical books of the four
temperaments and you will think you are reading
your own thoughts which you had not yet told.
Find the part which black eyes and which blue
eyes play severally in the company. How shall a
man escape from his ancestors, or draw off from
his veins the black drop which he drew from his
father's or his mother's life? It often appears in a
family as if all the qualities of the progenitors were
potted in several jars, — some ruling quality in each
son or daughter of the house; and sometimes the
unmixed temperament, the rank unmitigated elixir,
the family vice, is drawn off in a separate individual and the others are proportionally relieved.
We sometimes see a change of expression in our
companion and say his father or his mother comes
to the windows of his eyes, and sometimes a remote
relative. In different hours a man represents each
of several of his ancestors, as if there were seven
or eight of us rolled up in each man's skin, — seven
or eight ancestors at least; and they constitute
the variety of notes for that new piece of music
which his life is. At the corner of the street you
read the possibility of each passenger in the facial

angle, in the complexion, in the depth of his eye.
His parentage determines it. Men are what their
mothers made them. You may as well ask a loom
which weaves huckaback why it does not make
cashmere, as expect poetry from this engineer, or a
chemical discovery from that jobber. Ask the digger in the ditch to explain Newton's laws ; the fine
organs of his brain have been pinched by overwork
and squalid poverty from father to son for a hundred years. When each comes forth from his
mother's womb, the gate of gifts closes behind him.
Let him value his hands and feet, he has but one
pair. So he has but one future, and that is already
predetermined in his lobes and described in that
little fatty face, pig-eye, and squat form. All the
privilege and all the legislation of the world cannot meddle or help to make a poet or a prince of
him.

Jesus said, " When he looketh on her, he hath
committed adultery." But he is an adulterer before he has yet looked on the woman, by the super-
fluity of animal and the defect of thought in his
constitution. Who meets him, or who meets her,
in the street, sees that they are ripe to be each
other's victim.

In certain men digestion and sex absorb the vital
force, and the stronger these are, the individual is
so much weaker. The more of these drones perish,

the better for the hive. If, later, they give birth
to some superior individual, with force enough to
add to this animal a new aim and a complete apparatus to work it out, all the ancestors are gladly
forgotten.   Most men and most women are merely
one couple more.   Now and then one has a new
cell or camarilla opened in his brain, — an archi-
tectural, a musical, or a philological knack ; some
stray taste or talent for flowers, or chemistry, or
pigments, or story-telling; a good hand for draw-
ing, a good foot for dancing, an athletic frame for
wide journeying, &c. — which skill nowise alters
rank in the scale of nature, but serves to pass the
time ; the life of sensation going on as before.   At
last these hints and tendencies are fixed in one or
in a succession.   Each absorbs so much food and
force as to become itself a new centre.   The new
talent draws off so rapidly the vital force that not
enough remains for the animal functions, hardly
enough for health ; so that in the second generation, if the like genius appear, the health is visibly
deteriorated and the generative force impaired.

People are born with the moral or with the material bias ; — uterine brothers with this diverging
destination ; and I suppose, with high magnifiers,
Mr. Frauenhofer or Dr. Carpenter might come to
distinguish in the embryo, at the fourth day,—
this is a Whig, and that a Free-soiler.

It was a poetic attempt to lift this mountain of Fate, to reconcile this despotism of race with liberty, which led the Hindoos to say, "Fate is nothing but the deeds committed in a prior state of existence." I find the coincidence of the extremes of Eastern and Western speculation in the daring statement of Schelling, "There is in every man a certain feeling that he has been what he is from all eternity, and by no means became such in time." To say it less sublimely, — in the history of the individual is always an account of his condition, and he knows himself to be a party to his present estate.

A good deal of our politics is physiological. Now and then a man of wealth in the heyday of youth adopts the tenet of broadest freedom. In England there is always some man of wealth and large connection, planting himself, during all his years of health, on the side of progress, who, as soon as he begins to die, checks his forward play, calls in his troops and becomes conservative. All conservatives are such from personal defects. They have been effeminated by position or nature, born halt and blind, through luxury of their parents, and can only, like invalids, act on the defensive. But strong natures, backwoodsmen, New Hampshire giants, Napoleons, Burkes, Broughams, Websters, Kossuths, are inevitable patriots, until

their life ebbs and their defects and gout, palsy
and money, warp them.

The strongest idea incarnates itself in majorities
and nations, in the healthiest and strongest. Probably the election goes by avoirdupois weight, and
if you could weigh bodily the tonnage of any hundred of the Whig and the Democratic party in a
town on the Dearborn balance, as they passed the
hay-scales, you could predict with certainty which
party would carry it. On the whole it would be
rather the speediest way of deciding the vote, to
put the selectmen or the mayor and aldermen at
the hay-scales.

In science we have to consider two things;
power and circumstance. All we know of the egg,
from each successive discovery, is, *another vesicle;*
and if, after five hundred years you get a better
observer or a better glass, he finds, within the last
observed, another. In vegetable and animal tis-
sue it is just alike, and all that the primary power
or spasm operates is still vesicles, vesicles. Yes,
— but the tyrannical Circumstance! A vesicle
in new circumstances, a vesicle lodged in dark-
ness, Oken thought, became animal; in light, a
plant. Lodged in the parent animal, it suffers
changes which end in unsheathing miraculous ca-
pability in the unaltered vesicle, and it unlocks
itself to fish, bird, or quadruped, head and foot,

eye and claw.   The Circumstance is Nature.   Nature is what you may do.   There is much you may not.   We have two things, — the circumstance, and the life.   Once we thought positive power was all.   Now we learn that negative power, or circumstance, is half.   Nature is the tyrannous circumstance, the thick skull, the sheathed snake, the ponderous, rock-like jaw ; necessitated activity ; violent direction ; the conditions of a tool, like the locomotive, strong enough on its track, but which can do nothing but mischief off of it ; or skates, which are wings on the ice but fetters on the ground.

The book of Nature is the book of Fate.   She turns the gigantic pages, — leaf after leaf, — never re-turning one.   One leaf she lays down, a floor of granite ; then a thousand ages, and a bed of slate ; a thousand ages, and a measure of coal ; a thousand ages, and a layer of marl and mud : vegetable forms appear ; her first misshapen animals, zoöphyte, trilobium, fish ; then, saurians, — rude forms, in which she has only blocked her future statue, concealing under these unwieldly monsters the fine type of her coming king.   The face of the planet cools and dries, the races meliorate, and man is born.   But when a race has lived its term, it comes no more again.

The population of the world is a conditional

population; not the best, but the best that could live now; and the scale of tribes, and the steadiness with which victory adheres to one tribe and defeat to another, is as uniform as the superposition of strata. We know in history what weight belongs to race. We see the English, French, and Germans planting themselves on every shore and market of America and Australia, and monopolizing the commerce of these countries. We like the nervous and victorious habit of our own branch of the family. We follow the step of the Jew, of the Indian, of the Negro. We see how much will has been expended to extinguish the Jew, in vain. Look at the unpalatable conclusions of Knox, in his " Fragment of Races; " — a rash and unsatisfactory writer, but charged with pungent and unforgetable truths. " Nature respects race, and not hybrids." " Every race has its own *habitat.*" " Detach a colony from the race, and it deteriorates to the crab." See the shades of the picture. The German and Irish millions, like the Negro, have a great deal of guano in their destiny. They are ferried over the Atlantic and carted over America, to ditch and to drudge, to make corn cheap and then to lie down prematurely to make a spot of green grass on the prairie.

One more fagot of these adamantine bandages is the new science of Statistics. It is a rule that the most casual and extraordinary events, if the basis of population is broad enough, become matter of fixed calculation. It would not be safe to say when a captain like Bonaparte, a singer like Jenny Lind, or a navigator like Bowditch would be born in Boston; but, on a population of twenty or two hundred millions, something like accuracy may be had.[1]

'T is frivolous to fix pedantically the date of particular inventions. They have all been invented over and over fifty times. Man is the arch machine of which all these shifts drawn from himself are toy models. He helps himself on each emergency by copying or duplicating his own structure, just so far as the need is. 'T is hard to find the right Homer, Zoroaster, or Menu; harder still to find the Tubal Cain, or Vulcan, or Cadmus, or Copernicus, or Fust, or Fulton; the indisputable inventor. There are scores and centuries of them. " The air is full of men." This kind of talent so abounds, this constructive tool-making efficiency, as if it adhered to the chemic atoms; as if the air

[1] "Everything which pertains to the human species, considered as a whole, belongs to the order of physical facts. The greater the number of individuals, the more does the influence of the individual will disappear, leaving predominance to a series of general facts dependent on causes by which society exists, and is preserved." — QUETELET.

he breathes were made of Vaucansons, Franklins, and Watts.

Doubtless in every million there will be an astronomer, a mathematician, a comic poet, a mystic. No one can read the history of astronomy without perceiving that Copernicus, Newton, Laplace, are not new men, or a new kind of men, but that Thales, Anaximenes, Hipparchus, Empedocles, Aristarchus, Pythagoras, Œnipodes, had anticipated them; each had the same tense geometrical brain, apt for the same vigorous computation and logic; a mind parallel to the movement of the world. The Roman mile probably rested on a measure of a degree of the meridian. Mahometan and Chinese know what we know of leap-year, of the Gregorian calendar, and of the precession of the equinoxes. As in every barrel of cowries brought to New Bedford there shall be one *orangia*, so there will, in a dozen millions of Malays and Mahometans, be one or two astronomical skulls. In a large city, the most casual things, and things whose beauty lies in their casualty, are produced as punctually and to order as the baker's muffin for breakfast. Punch makes exactly one capital joke a week; and the journals contrive to furnish one good piece of news every day.

And not less work the laws of repression, the penalties of violated functions. Famine, typhus,

frost, war, suicide and effete races must be reckoned calculable parts of the system of the world.

These are pebbles from the mountain, hints of
the terms by which our life is walled up, and which
show a kind of mechanical exactness, as of a loom
or mill, in what we call casual or fortuitous events.

The force with which we resist these torrents of
tendency looks so ridiculously inadequate that it
amounts to little more than a criticism or a protest
made by a minority of one, under compulsion of
millions. I seemed in the height of a tempest to
see men overboard struggling in the waves, and
driven about here and there. They glanced intelligently at each other, but 't was little they could do
for one another ; 't was much if each could keep
afloat alone. Well, they had a right to their eye-
beams, and all the rest was Fate.

We cannot trifle with this reality, this cropping-
out in our planted gardens of the core of the world.
No picture of life can have any veracity that does
not admit the odious facts. A man's power is
hooped in by a necessity which, by many experiments, he touches on every side until he learns its
arc.

The element running through entire nature,
which we popularly call Fate, is known to us as
limitation. Whatever limits us we call Fate. If

we are brute and barbarous, the fate takes a brute and dreadful shape. As we refine, our checks become finer. If we rise to spiritual culture, the antagonism takes a spiritual form. In the Hindoo fables, Vishnu follows Maya through all her ascending changes, from insect and crawfish up to elephant; whatever form she took, he took the male form of that kind, until she became at last woman and goddess, and he a man and a god. The limitations refine as the soul purifies, but the ring of necessity is always perched at the top.

When the gods in the Norse heaven were unable to bind the Fenris Wolf with steel or with weight of mountains, — the one he snapped and the other he spurned with his heel, — they put round his foot a limp band softer than silk or cobweb, and this held him; the more he spurned it the stiffer it drew. So soft and so stanch is the ring of Fate. Neither brandy, nor nectar, nor sulphuric ether, nor hell-fire, nor ichor, nor poetry, nor genius, can get rid of this limp band. For if we give it the high sense in which the poets use it, even thought itself is not above Fate; that too must act according to eternal laws, and all that is wilful and fantastic in it is in opposition to its fundamental essence.

And last of all, high over thought, in the world of morals, Fate appears as vindicator, levelling the

high, lifting the low, requiring justice in man,
and always striking soon or late when justice is
not done. What is useful will last; what is hurtful will sink. "The doer must suffer," said the
Greeks; "you would soothe a Deity not to be
soothed." "God himself cannot procure good for
the wicked," said the Welsh triad. "God may
consent, but only for a time," said the bard of
Spain. The limitation is impassable by any insight of man. In its last and loftiest ascensions,
insight itself and the freedom of the will is one
of its obedient members. But we must not run
into generalizations too large, but show the natural bounds or essential distinctions, and seek to
do justice to the other elements as well.

Thus we trace Fate in matter, mind, and morals;
in race, in retardations of strata, and in thought
and character as well. It is everywhere bound or
limitation. But Fate has its lord; limitation its
limits, — is different seen from above and from
below, from within and from without. For though
Fate is immense, so is Power, which is the other
fact in the dual world, immense. If Fate follows
and limits Power, Power attends and antagonizes
Fate. We must respect Fate as natural history,
but there is more than natural history. For who
and what is this criticism that pries into the mat-

ter? Man is not order of nature, sack and sack,
belly and members, link in a chain, nor any igno-
minious baggage; but a stupendous antagonism, a
dragging together of the poles of the Universe. He
betrays his relation to what is below him, — thick-
skulled, small-brained, fishy, quadrumanous, quadruped ill-disguised, hardly escaped into biped, —
and has paid for the new powers by loss of some of
the old ones. But the lightning which explodes
and fashions planets, maker of planets and suns, is
in him. On one side elemental order, sandstone
and granite, rock-ledges, peat-bog, forest, sea and
shore; and on the other part thought, the spirit
which composes and decomposes nature, — here
they are, side by side, god and devil, mind and
matter, king and conspirator, belt and spasm, riding peacefully together in the eye and brain of
every man.

Nor can he blink the freewill. To hazard the
contradiction, — freedom is necessary. If you
please to plant yourself on the side of Fate, and
say, Fate is all; then we say, a part of Fate is the
freedom of man. Forever wells up the impulse
of choosing and acting in the soul. Intellect an-
nuls Fate. So far as a man thinks, he is free.
And though nothing is more disgusting than the
crowing about liberty by slaves, as most men are,
and the flippant mistaking for freedom of some

paper preamble like a " Declaration of Independence " or the statute right to vote, by those who have never dared to think or to act, — yet it is wholesome to man to look not at Fate, but the other way: the practical view is the other. His sound relation to these facts is to use and command, not to cringe to them. " Look not on Nature, for her name is fatal," said the oracle. The too much contemplation of these limits induces meanness. They who talk much of destiny, their birth-star, &c., are in a lower dangerous plane, and invite the evils they fear.

I cited the instinctive and heroic races as proud believers in Destiny. They conspire with it; a loving resignation is with the event. But the dogma makes a different impression when it is held by the weak and lazy. 'T is weak and vicious people who cast the blame on Fate. The right use of Fate is to bring up our conduct to the loftiness of nature. Rude and invincible except by themselves are the elements. So let man be. Let him empty his breast of his windy conceits, and show his lordship by manners and deeds on the scale of nature. Let him hold his purpose as with the tug of gravitation. No power, no persuasion, no bribe shall make him give up his point. A man ought to compare advantageously with a river, an oak, or a mountain. He shall have not less the flow, the expansion, and the resistance of these.

'T is the best use of Fate to teach a fatal courage. Go face the fire at sea, or the cholera in your friend's house, or the burglar in your own, or what danger lies in the way of duty, — knowing you are guarded by the cherubim of Destiny. If you believe in Fate to your harm, believe it at least for your good.

For if Fate is so prevailing, man also is part of it, and can confront fate with fate. If the Universe have these savage accidents, our atoms are as savage in resistance. We should be crushed by the atmosphere, but for the reaction of the air within the body. A tube made of a film of glass can resist the shock of the ocean if filled with the same water. If there be omnipotence in the stroke, there is omnipotence of recoil.

1. But Fate against Fate is only parrying and defence: there are also the noble creative forces. The revelation of Thought takes man out of servitude into freedom. We rightly say of ourselves, we were born and afterward we were born again, and many times. We have successive experiences so important that the new forgets the old, and hence the mythology of the seven or the nine heavens. The day of days, the great day of the feast of life, is that in which the inward eye opens to

the Unity in things, to the omnipresence of law:
— sees that what is must be and ought to be, or is
the best. This beatitude dips from on high down
on us and we see. It is not in us so much as we
are in it. If the air come to our lungs, we breathe
and live; if not, we die. If the light come to our
eyes, we see; else not. And if truth come to our
mind we suddenly expand to its dimensions, as if
we grew to worlds. We are as lawgivers; we
speak for Nature; we prophesy and divine.

This insight throws us on the party and interest
of the Universe, against all and sundry; against
ourselves as much as others. A man speaking
from insight affirms of himself what is true of the
mind: seeing its immortality, he says, I am immortal; seeing its invincibility, he says, I am strong.
It is not in us, but we are in it. It is of the
maker, not of what is made. All things are
touched and changed by it. This uses and is not
used. It distances those who share it from those
who share it not. Those who share it not are
flocks and herds. It dates from itself; not from
former men or better men, gospel, or constitution,
or college, or custom. Where it shines, Nature is
no longer intrusive, but all things make a musical
or pictorial impression. The world of men show
like a comedy without laughter: populations, interests, government, history; 't is all toy figures in a

toy house. It does not over value particular truths.
We hear eagerly every thought and word quoted
from an intellectual man.   But in his presence our
own mind is roused to activity, and we forget very
fast what he says, much more interested in the new
play of our own thought than in any thought of
his.   'T is the majesty into which we have suddenly
mounted, the impersonality, the scorn of egotisms,
the sphere of laws, that engage us.   Once we were
stepping a little this way and a little that way ;
now we are as men in a balloon, and do not think
so much of the point we have left, or the point we
would make, as of the liberty and glory of the
way.

Just as much intellect as you add, so much organic power. He who sees through the design, pre-
sides over it, and must will that which must be.
We sit and rule, and, though we sleep, our dream
will come to pass. Our thought, though it were
only an hour old, affirms an oldest necessity, not to
be separated from thought, and not to be separated
from will. They must always have coexisted. It
apprises us of its sovereignty and godhead, which
refuse to be severed from it. It is not mine or
thine, but the will of all mind. It is poured into
the souls of all men, as the soul itself which constitutes them men. I know not whether there be, as
is alleged, in the upper region of our atmosphere, a

permanent westerly current which carries with it
all atoms which rise to that height, but I see that
when souls reach a certain clearness of perception
they accept a knowledge and motive above selfishness.   A breath of will blows eternally through
the universe of souls in the direction of the Right
and Necessary.   It is the air which all intellects ·
inhale and exhale, and it is the wind which blows
the worlds into order and orbit.

Thought dissolves the material universe by carrying the mind up into a sphere where all is plas-
tic.   Of two men, each obeying his own thought,
he whose thought is deepest will be the strongest
character.   Always one man more than another
represents the will of Divine Providence to the
period.

2. If thought makes free, so does the moral sentiment.   The mixtures of spiritual chemistry refuse to be analyzed.   Yet we can see that with the
perception of truth is joined the desire that it shall
prevail ; that affection is essential to will.   Moreover, when a strong will appears, it usually results
from a certain unity of organization, as if the whole
energy of body and mind flowed in one direction.
All great force is real and elemental.   There is
no manufacturing a strong will.   There must be a
pound to balance a pound.   Where power is shown
in will, it must rest on the universal force.   Alaric

and Bonaparte must believe they rest on a truth, or their will can be bought or bent. There is a bribe possible for any finite will. But the pure sympathy with universal ends is an infinite force, and cannot be bribed or bent. Whoever has had experience of the moral sentiment cannot choose but believe in unlimited power. Each pulse from that heart is an oath from the Most High. I know not what the word *sublime* means, if it be not the intimations, in this infant, of a terrific force. A text of heroism, a name and anecdote of courage, are not arguments but sallies of freedom. One of these is the verse of the Persian Hafiz, " 'T is written on the gate of Heaven, ' Woe unto him who suffers himself to be betrayed by Fate!' " Does the reading of history make us fatalists? What courage does not the opposite opinion show! A little whim of will to be free gallantly contending against the universe of chemistry.

But insight is not will, nor is affection will. Perception is cold, and goodness dies in wishes. As Voltaire said, 't is the misfortune of worthy people that they are cowards ; " *un des plus grands malheurs des honnêtes gens c'est qu'ils sont des lâches.*" There must be a fusion of these two to generate the energy of will. There can be no driving force except through the conversion of the man into his will, making him the will, and the

will him. And one may say boldly that no man
has a right perception of any truth who has not
been reacted on by it so as to be ready to be its
martyr.

The one serious and formidable thing in nature
is a will. Society is servile from want of will, and
therefore the world wants saviours and religions.
One way is right to go; the hero sees it, and
moves on that aim, and has the world under him
for root and support. He is to others as the world.
His approbation is honor; his dissent, infamy. The
glance of his eye has the force of sunbeams. A
personal influence towers up in memory only worthy, and we gladly forget numbers, money, climate,
gravitation, and the rest of Fate.

We can afford to allow the limitation, if we
know it is the meter of the growing man. We
stand against Fate, as children stand up against the
wall in their father's house and notch their height
from year to year. But when the boy grows to
man, and is master of the house, he pulls down that
wall and builds a new and bigger. 'T is only a
question of time. Every brave youth is in training to ride and rule this dragon. His science is
to make weapons and wings of these passions and
retarding forces. Now whether, seeing these two
things, fate and power, we are permitted to believe

in unity? The bulk of mankind believe in two gods. They are under one dominion here in the house, as friend and parent, in social circles, in letters, in art, in love, in religion ; but in mechanics, in dealing with steam and climate, in trade, in politics, they think they come under another ; and that it would be a practical blunder to transfer the method and way of working of one sphere into the other. What good, honest, generous men at home, will be wolves and foxes on 'Change! What pious men in the parlor will vote for what reprobates at the polls! To a certain point, they believe themselves the care of a Providence. But in a steamboat, in an epidemic, in war, they believe a malignant energy rules.

But relation and connection are not somewhere and sometimes, but everywhere and always. The divine order does not stop where their sight stops. The friendly power works on the same rules in the next farm and the next planet. But where they have not experience they run against it and hurt themselves. Fate then is a name for facts not yet passed under the fire of thought ; for causes which are unpenetrated.

But every jet of chaos which threatens to exterminate us is convertible by intellect into wholesome force. Fate is unpenetrated causes. The water drowns ship and sailor like a grain of dust. But learn to swim, trim your bark, and the wave which drowned it will be cloven by it and carry it like its own foam, a plume and a power. The cold is inconsiderate of persons, tingles your blood, freezes a man like a dew-drop. But learn to skate, and the ice will give you a graceful, sweet, and poetic motion. The cold will brace your limbs and brain to genius, and make you foremost men of time. Cold and sea will train an imperial Saxon race, which nature cannot bear to lose, and after cooping it up for a thousand years in yonder England, gives a hundred Englands, a hundred Mexicos. All the bloods it shall absorb and domineer: and more than Mexicos, the secrets of water and steam, the spasms of electricity, the ductility of metals, the chariot of the air, the ruddered balloon are awaiting you.

The annual slaughter from typhus far exceeds that of war; but right drainage destroys typhus. The plague in the sea-service from scurvy is healed. by lemon juice and other diets portable or procurable; the depopulation by cholera and small-pox is ended by drainage and vaccination; and every other pest is not less in the chain of cause and effect, and may be fought off. And whilst art draws out the venom, it commonly extorts some benefit from the vanquished enemy. The mischievous torrent is taught to drudge for man; the wild beasts he makes useful for food, or dress, or labor; the chemic explosions are controlled like his watch. These are now the steeds on which he rides. Man moves in all modes, by legs of horses, by wings of wind, by steam, by gas of balloon, by electricity, and stands on tiptoe threatening to hunt the eagle in his own element. There's nothing he will not make his carrier.

Steam was till the other day the devil which we dreaded. Every pot made by any human potter or brazier had a hole in its cover, to let off the enemy, lest he should lift pot and roof and carry the house away. But the Marquis of Worcester, Watt, and Fulton bethought themselves that where was power was not devil, but was God; that it must be availed of, and not by any means let off and wasted. Could he lift pots and roofs and houses so handily? He was the workman they were in search of. He could be used to lift away, chain and compel other devils far more reluctant and dangerous, namely cubic miles of earth, mountains, weight or resistance of water, machinery, and the labors of all men in the world; and time he shall lengthen, and shorten space.

It has not fared much otherwise with higher kinds of steam. The opinion of the million was the terror of the world, and it was attempted either to dissipate it, by amusing nations, or to pile it over with strata of society, — a layer of soldiers, over that a layer of lords, and a king on the top; with clamps and hoops of castles, garrisons, and police. But sometimes the religious principle would get in and burst the hoops and rive every mountain laid on top of it. The Fultons and Watts of politics, believing in unity, saw that it was a power, and by satisfying it (as justice satisfies everybody), through a different disposition of society, — grouping it on a level instead of piling it into a mountain, — they have contrived to make of this terror the most harmless and energetic form of a State.

Very odious, I confess, are the lessons of Fate. Who likes to have a dapper phrenologist pronouncing on his fortunes? Who likes to believe that he has, hidden in his skull, spine, and pelvis, all the vices of a Saxon or Celtic race, which will be sure to pull him down, — with what grandeur of hope and resolve he is fired, — into a selfish, huckstering, servile, dodging animal? A learned physician tells us the fact is invariable with the Neapolitan, that when mature he assumes the forms of the unmistakable scoundrel. That is a little overstated, — but may pass.

But these are magazines and arsenals. A man must thank his defects, and stand in some terror of his talents. A transcendent talent draws so largely on his forces as to lame him; a defect pays him revenues on the other side. The sufferance which is the badge of the Jew, has made him, in these days, the ruler of the rulers of the earth. If Fate is ore and quarry, if evil is good in the making, if limitation is power that shall be, if calamities, oppositions, and weights are wings and means, — we are reconciled.

Fate involves the melioration. No statement of the Universe can have any soundness which does not admit its ascending effort. The direction of the whole and of the parts is toward benefit, and in proportion to the health. Behind every individual closes organization; before him opens liberty, — the Better, the Best. The first and worse races are dead. The second and imperfect races are dying out, or remain for the maturing of higher. In the latest race, in man, every generosity, every new perception, the love and praise he extorts from his fellows, are certificates of advance out of fate into freedom. Liberation of the will from the sheaths and clogs of organization which he has outgrown, is the end and aim of this world. Every calamity is a spur and valuable hint; and where his endeavors do not yet fully avail, they tell as tendency. The whole circle of animal life, — tooth against tooth, devouring war, war for food, a yelp of pain and a grunt of triumph, until at last the whole menagerie, the whole chemical mass is mellowed and refined for higher use, — pleases at a sufficient perspective.

But to see how fate slides into freedom and freedom into fate, observe how far the roots of every creature run, or find if you can a point where there is no thread of connection. Our life is consentaneous and far-related. This knot of nature is so well tied that nobody was ever cunning enough to find the two ends. Nature is intricate, over-lapped, interweaved and endless. Christopher Wren said of the beautiful King's College chapel, that " if anybody would tell him where to lay the first stone, he would build such another." But where shall we find the first atom in this house of man, which is all consent, inosculation, and balance of parts?

The web of relation is shown in *habitat*, shown in hibernation. When hibernation was observed, it was found that whilst some animals became torpid in winter, others were torpid in summer : hibernation then was a false name. The *long sleep* is not an effect of cold, but is regulated by the supply of food proper to the animal. It becomes torpid when the fruit or prey it lives on is not in season, and regains its activity when its food is ready.

Eyes are found in light ; ears in auricular air ; feet on land ; fins in water ; wings in air ; and each creature where it was meant to be, with a mutual

fitness. Every zone has its own *Fauna*. There
is adjustment between the animal and its food, its
parasite, its enemy. Balances are kept. It is not
allowed to diminish in numbers, nor to exceed.
The like adjustments exist for man. His food is
cooked when he arrives ; his coal in the pit ; the
house ventilated ; the mud of the deluge dried ; his
companions arrived at the same hour, and awaiting
him with love, concert, laughter and tears. These
are coarse adjustments, but the invisible are not
less. There are more belongings to every creature
than his air and his food. His instincts must be
met, and he has predisposing power that bends and
fits what is near him to his use. He is not possible until the invisible things are right for him, as
well as the visible. Of what changes then in sky
and earth, and in finer skies and earths, does the
appearance of some Dante or Columbus apprise
us !

How is this effected ? Nature is no spendthrift,
but takes the shortest way to her ends. As the
general says to his soldiers, " If you want a fort,
build a fort," so nature makes every creature do its
own work and get its living, — is it planet, animal
or tree. The planet makes itself. The animal cell
makes itself ; — then, what it wants. Every creature, wren or dragon, shall make its own lair. As
soon as there is life, there is self-direction and ab-

sorbing and using of material. Life is freedom, —
life in the direct ratio of its amount. You may be
sure the new-born man is not inert. Life works
both voluntarily and supernaturally in its neighborhood. Do you suppose he can be estimated by his
weight in pounds, or that he is contained in his
skin, — this reaching, radiating, jaculating fellow?
The smallest candle fills a mile with its rays, and
the papillæ of a man run out to every star.

When there is something to be done, the world
knows how to get it done. The vegetable eye
makes leaf, pericarp, root, bark, or thorn, as the
need is; the first cell converts itself into stomach,
mouth, nose, or nail, according to the want; the
world throws its life into a hero or a shepherd, and
puts him where he is wanted. Dante and Columbus were Italians, in their time; they would be
Russians or Americans to-day. Things ripen, new
men come. The adaptation is not capricious. The
ulterior aim, the purpose beyond itself, the correlation by which planets subside and crystallize,
then animate beasts and men, — will not stop but
will work into finer particulars, and from finer to
finest.

The secret of the world is the tie between person
and event. Person makes event, and event person.
The "times," "the age," what is that but a few
profound persons and a few active persons who

epitomize the times?—Goethe, Hegel, Metternich,
Adams, Calhoun, Guizot, Peel, Cobden, Kossuth,
Rothschild, Astor, Brunel, and the rest. The same
fitness must be presumed between a man and the
time and event, as between the sexes, or between a
race of animals and the food it eats, or the inferior
races it uses. He thinks his fate alien, because the
copula is hidden. But the soul contains the event
that shall befall it; for the event is only the actual-
ization of its thoughts, and what we pray to ourselves for is always granted. The event is the print
of your form. It fits you like your skin. What
each does is proper to him. Events are the children
of his body and mind. We learn that the soul of
Fate is the soul of us, as Hafiz sings, —

> " Alas ! till now I had not known,
>   My guide and fortune's guide are one."

All the toys that infatuate men and which they
play for, — houses, land, money, luxury, power,
fame, are the selfsame thing, with a new gauze or
two of illusion overlaid. And of all the drums
and rattles by which men are made willing to have
their heads broke, and are led out solemnly every
morning to parade, — the most admirable is this
by which we are brought to believe that events are
arbitrary and independent of actions. At the con-
juror's, we detect the hair by which he moves his

puppet, but we have not eyes sharp enough to descry the thread that ties cause and effect.

Nature magically suits the man to his fortunes, by making these the fruit of his character. Ducks take to the water, eagles to the sky, waders to the sea margin, hunters to the forest, clerks to counting-rooms, soldiers to the frontier. Thus events grow on the same stem with persons; are sub-persons. The pleasure of life is according to the man that lives it, and not according to the work or the place. Life is an ecstasy. We know what madness belongs to love, — what power to paint a vile object in hues of heaven. As insane persons are indifferent to their dress, diet, and other accommodations, and as we do in dreams, with equanimity, the most absurd acts, so a drop more of wine in our cup of life will reconcile us to strange company and work. Each creature puts forth from itself its own condition and sphere, as the slug sweats out its slimy house on the pear-leaf, and the woolly aphides on the apple perspire their own bed, and the fish its shell. In youth we clothe ourselves with rainbows and go as brave as the zodiac. In age we put out another sort of perspiration, — gout, fever, rheumatism, caprice, doubt, fretting and avarice.

A man's fortunes are the fruit of his character. A man's friends are his magnetisms. We go to Herodotus and Plutarch for examples of Fate; but

we are examples. " *Quisque suos patimur manes.*"
The tendency of every man to enact all that is in
his constitution is expressed in the old belief that
the efforts which we make to escape from our destiny only serve to lead us into it: and I have noticed a man likes better to be complimented on his
position, as the proof of the last or total excellence,
than on his merits.

A man will see his character emitted in the
events that seem to meet, but which exude from
and accompany him. Events expand with the character. As once he found himself among toys, so
now he plays a part in colossal systems, and his
growth is declared in his ambition, his companions
and his performance. He looks like a piece of luck,
but is a piece of causation; the mosaic, angulated
and ground to fit into the gap he fills. Hence in
each town there is some man who is, in his brain
and performance, an explanation of the tillage, production, factories, banks, churches, ways of living
and society of that town. If you do not chance to
meet him, all that you see will leave you a little
puzzled; if you see him it will become plain. We
know in Massachusetts who built New Bedford, who
built Lynn, Lowell, Lawrence, Clinton, Fitchburg,
Holyoke, Portland, and many another noisy mart.
Each of these men, if they were transparent, would
seem to you not so much men as walking cities, and
wherever you put them they would build one.

History is the action and reaction of these two, — Nature and Thought; two boys pushing each other on the curbstone of the pavement. Everything is pusher or pushed; and matter and mind are in perpetual tilt and balance, so. Whilst the man is weak, the earth takes up him. He plants his brain and affections. By and by he will take up the earth, and have his gardens and vineyards in the beautiful order and productiveness of his thought. Every solid in the universe is ready to become fluid on the approach of the mind, and the power to flux it is the measure of the mind. If the wall remain adamant, it accuses the want of thought. To a subtler force it will stream into new forms, expressive of the character of the mind. What is the city in which we sit here, but an aggregate of incongruous materials which have obeyed the will of some man? The granite was reluctant, but his hands were stronger, and it came. Iron was deep in the ground and well combined with stone, but could not hide from his fires. Wood, lime, stuffs, fruits, gums, were dispersed over the earth and sea, in vain. Here they are, within reach of every man's day-labor, — what he wants of them. The whole world is the flux of matter over the wires of thought to the poles or points where it would build. The races of men rise out of the ground preoccupied with a thought which rules

them, and divided into parties ready armed and
angry to fight for this metaphysical abstraction.
The quality of the thought differences the Egyptian and the Roman, the Austrian and the American. The men who come on the stage at one
period are all found to be related to each other.
Certain ideas are in the air. We are all impressionable, for we are made of them; all impressionable, but some more than others, and these first express them. This explains the curious contempora-
neousness of inventions and discoveries. The truth
is in the air, and the most impressionable brain
will announce it first, but all will announce it a few
minutes later. So women, as most susceptible, are
the best index of the coming hour. So the great
man, that is, the man most imbued with the spirit of
the time, is the impressionable man; — of a fibre
irritable and delicate, like iodine to light. He feels
the infinitesimal attractions. His mind is righter
than others because he yields to a current so feeble
as can be felt only by a needle delicately poised.

The correlation is shown in defects. Möller, in
his Essay on Architecture, taught that the building which was fitted accurately to answer its end
would turn out to be beautiful though beauty had
not been intended. I find the like unity in human
structures rather virulent and pervasive; that a
crudity in the blood will appear in the argument;

a hump in the shoulder will appear in the speech and handiwork. If his mind could be seen, the hump would be seen. If a man has a seesaw in his voice, it will run into his sentences, into his poem, into the structure of his fable, into his speculation, into his charity. And as every man is hunted by his own dæmon, vexed by his own disease, this checks all his activity.

So each man, like each plant, has his parasites. A strong, astringent, bilious nature has more truculent enemies than the slugs and moths that fret my leaves. Such an one has curculios, borers, knife-worms; a swindler ate him first, then a client, then a quack, then smooth, plausible gentlemen, bitter and selfish as Moloch.

This correlation really existing can be divined. If the threads are there, thought can follow and show them. Especially when a soul is quick and docile, as Chaucer sings; —

> " Or if the soul of proper kind
>   Be so perfect as men find,
>   That it wot what is to come,
>   And that he warneth all and some
>   Of every of their aventures,
>   By previsions or figures ;
>   But that our flesh hath not might
>   It to understand aright
>   For it is warned too darkly."

Some people are made up of rhyme, coincidence,

omen, periodicity, and presage : they meet the person they seek; what their companion prepares to
say to them, they first say to him; and a hundred
signs apprise them of what is about to befall.

Wonderful intricacy in the web, wonderful constancy in the design this vagabond life admits.
We wonder how the fly finds its mate, and yet
year after year, we find two men, two women,
without legal or carnal tie, spend a great part of
their best time within a few feet of each other.
And the moral is that what we seek we shall find;
what we flee from flees from us; as Goethe said,
"what we wish for in youth, comes in heaps on us
in old age," too often cursed with the granting of
our prayer: and hence the high caution, that since
we are sure of having what we wish, we beware to
ask only for high things.

One key, one solution to the mysteries of human
condition, one solution to the old knots of fate,
freedom, and foreknowledge, exists; the propound-
ing, namely, of the double consciousness. A man
must ride alternately on the horses of his private
and his public nature, as the equestrians in the
circus throw themselves nimbly from horse to
horse, or plant one foot on the back of one and
the other foot on the back of the other. So when
a man is the victim of his fate, has sciatica in his
loins and cramp in his mind; a club-foot and a

club in his wit; a sour face and a selfish temper;
a strut in his gait and a conceit in his affection;
or is ground to powder by the vice of his race; —
he is to rally on his relation to the Universe,
which his ruin benefits. Leaving the dæmon who
suffers, he is to take sides with the Deity who secures universal benefit by his pain.

To offset the drag of temperament and race,
which pulls down, learn this lesson, namely that
by the cunning co-presence of two elements, which
is throughout nature, whatever lames or paralyzes
you draws in with it the divinity, in some form,
to repay. A good intention clothes itself with
sudden power. When a god wishes to ride, any
chip or pebble will bud and shoot out winged feet
and serve him for a horse.

Let us build altars to the Blessed Unity which
holds nature and souls in perfect solution, and com-
pels every atom to serve an universal end. I do
not wonder at a snow-flake, a shell, a summer landscape, or the glory of the stars; but at the necessity
of beauty under which the universe lies; that all
is and must be pictorial; that the rainbow and the
curve of the horizon and the arch of the blue vault
are only results from the organism of the eye.
There is no need for foolish amateurs to fetch me
to admire a garden of flowers, or a sun-gilt cloud,
or a waterfall, when I cannot look without seeing

splendor and grace. How idle to choose a random sparkle here or there, when the indwelling necessity plants the rose of beauty on the brow of chaos, and discloses the central intention of Nature to be harmony and joy.

Let us build altars to the Beautiful Necessity. If we thought men were free in the sense that in a single exception one fantastical will could prevail over the law of things, it were all one as if a child's hand could pull down the sun. If in the least particular one could derange the order of nature, — who would accept the gift of life?

Let us build altars to the Beautiful Necessity, which secures that all is made of one piece; that plaintiff and defendant, friend and enemy, animal and planet, food and eater are of one kind. In astronomy is vast space but no foreign system; in geology, vast time but the same laws as to-day. Why should we be afraid of Nature, which is no other than " philosophy and theology embodied " ? Why should we fear to be crushed by savage elements, we who are made up of the same elements? Let us build to the Beautiful Necessity, which makes man brave in believing that he cannot shun a danger that is appointed, nor incur one that is not ; to the Necessity which rudely or softly educates him to the perception that there are no contingencies ; that Law rules throughout existence ; a Law which is not intelligent but intelligence ; — not personal nor impersonal — it disdains words and passes understanding; it dissolves persons; it vivifies nature; yet solicits the pure in heart to draw on all its omnipotence.

II.

POWER.

———◆———

His tongue was framed to music,
And his hand was armed with skill;
His face was the mould of beauty,
And his heart the throne of will.

POWER.

THERE is not yet any inventory of a man's faculties, any more than a bible of his opinions. Who shall set a limit to the influence of a human being? There are men who by their sympathetic attractions carry nations with them and lead the activity of the human race. And if there be such a tie that wherever the mind of man goes, nature will accompany him, perhaps there are men whose magnetisms are of that force to draw material and elemental powers, and, where they appear, immense instrumentalities organize around them. Life is a search after power; and this is an element with which the world is so saturated, — there is no chink or crevice in which it is not lodged, — that no honest seeking goes unrewarded. A man should prize events and possessions as the ore in which this fine mineral is found; and he can well afford to let events and possessions and the breath of the body go, if their value has been added to him in the shape of power. If he have secured the elixir, he can spare the wide gardens from which it was distilled. A cultivated man, wise to know and bold to perform, is the end to which Nature works, and

the education of the will is the flowering and re
sult of all this geology and astronomy.

All successful men have agreed in one thing, —
they were *causationists*. They believed that things
went not by luck, but by law; that there was not
a weak or a cracked link in the chain that joins
the first and last of things. A belief in causality,
or strict connection between every pulse-beat and
the principle of being, and, in consequence, belief
in compensation, or that nothing is got for nothing,
— characterizes all valuable minds, and must control every effort that is made by an industrious
one. The most valiant men are the best believers
in the tension of the laws. "All the great cap-
tains," said Bonaparte, "have performed vast
achievements by conforming with the rules of the
art, — by adjusting efforts to obstacles."

The key to the age may be this, or that, or the
other, as the young orators describe; the key to
all ages is — Imbecility; imbecility in the vast
majority of men at all times, and even in heroes
in all but certain eminent moments; victims of
gravity, custom, and fear. This gives force to the
strong, — that the multitude have no habit of self-
reliance or original action.

We must reckon success a constitutional trait.
Courage, the old physicians taught (and their
meaning holds, if their physiology is a little myth-

ical), — courage, or the degree of life, is as the degree of circulation of the blood in the arteries. "During passion, anger, fury, trials of strength, wrestling, fighting, a large amount of blood is collected in the arteries, the maintenance of bodily strength requiring it, and but little is sent into the veins. This condition is constant with intrepid persons." Where the arteries hold their blood, is courage and adventure possible. Where they pour it unrestrained into the veins, the spirit is low and feeble. For performance of great mark, it needs extraordinary health. If Eric is in robust health, and has slept well, and is at the top of his condition, and thirty years old, at his departure from Greenland he will steer west, and his ships will reach Newfoundland. But take out Eric and put in a stronger and bolder man, — Biorn, or Thorfin, — and the ships will, with just as much ease, sail six hundred, one thousand, fifteen hundred miles further, and reach Labrador and New England. There is no chance in results. With adults, as with children, one class enter cordially into the game and whirl with the whirling world; the others have cold hands and remain bystanders; or are only dragged in by the humor and vivacity of those who can carry a dead weight. The first wealth is health. Sickness is poor-spirited, and cannot serve any one : it must husband its resources to live. But

health or fulness answers its own ends and has to
spare, runs over, and inundates the neighborhoods
and creeks of other men's necessities.

All power is of one kind, a sharing of the nature
of the world. The mind that is parallel with the
laws of nature will be in the current of events and
strong with their strength. One man is made of
the same stuff of which events are made; is in
sympathy with the course of things; can predict it.
Whatever befalls, befalls him first; so that he is
equal to whatever shall happen. A man who knows
men, can talk well on politics, trade, law, war, religion. For everywhere men are led in the same
manners.

The advantage of a strong pulse is not to be supplied by any labor, art, or concert. It is like the
climate, which easily rears a crop which no glass,
or irrigation, or tillage, or manures can elsewhere
rival. It is like the opportunity of a city like New
York or Constantinople, which needs no diplomacy
to force capital or genius or labor to it. They come
of themselves, as the waters flow to it. So a broad,
healthy, massive understanding seems to lie on the
shore of unseen rivers, of unseen oceans, which are
covered with barks that night and day are drifted
to this point. That is poured into its lap which
other men lie plotting for. It is in everybody's
secret; anticipates everybody's discovery; and if it

do not command every fact of the genius and the scholar, it is because it is large and sluggish, and does not think them worth the exertion which you do.

This affirmative force is in one and is not in another, as one horse has the spring in him, and another in the whip. "On the neck of the young man," said Hafiz, "sparkles no gem so gracious as enterprise." Import into any stationary district, as into an old Dutch population in New York or Pennsylvania, or among the planters of Virginia, a colony of hardy Yankees, with seething brains, heads full of steam-hammer, pulley, crank, and toothed wheel, — and everything begins to shine with values. What enhancement to all the water and land in England is the arrival of James Watt or Brunel! In every company there is not only the active and passive sex, but in both men and women a deeper and more important *sex of mind*, namely the inventive or creative class of both men and women, and the uninventive or accepting class. Each *plus* man represents his set, and if he have the accidental advantage of personal ascendency, — which implies neither more nor less of talent, but merely the temperamental or taming eye of a soldier or a schoolmaster (which one has, and one has not, as one has a black moustache and one a blonde), — then quite easily and without envy or resistance all his coadjutors and feeders will admit his right to absorb them. The merchant works by book-keeper and cashier; the lawyer's authorities are hunted up by clerks; the geologist reports the surveys of his subalterns; Commander Wilkes appropriates the results of all the naturalists attached to the Expedition; Thorwaldsen's statue is finished by stone-cutters; Dumas has journeymen; and Shakspeare was theatre-manager and used the labor of many young men, as well as the playbooks.

There is always room for a man of force, and he makes room for many. Society is a troop of thinkers, and the best heads among them take the best places. A feeble man can see the farms that are fenced and tilled, the houses that are built. The strong man sees the possible houses and farms. His eye makes estates, as fast as the sun breeds clouds.

When a new boy comes into school, when a man travels and encounters strangers every day, or when into any old club a new comer is domesticated, — that happens which befalls when a strange ox is driven into a pen or pasture where cattle are kept; there is at once a trial of strength between the best pair of horns and the new comer, and it is settled thenceforth which is the leader. So now, there is a measuring of strength, very courteous but decisive, and an acquiescence thence-

forward when these two meet. Each reads his fate
in the other's eyes. The weaker party finds that
none of his information or wit quite fits the occasion. He thought he knew this or that; he finds
that he omitted to learn the end of it. Nothing
that he knows will quite hit the mark, whilst all
the rival's arrows are good, and well thrown. But
if he knew all the facts in the encyclopedia, it
would not help him; for this is an affair of presence of mind, of attitude, of aplomb: the opponent
has the sun and wind, and, in every cast, the choice
of weapon and mark; and when he himself is
matched with some other antagonist, his own shafts
fly well and hit. 'T is a question of stomach and
constitution. The second man is as good as the
first, — perhaps better; but has not stoutness or
stomach, as the first has, and so his wit seems over-
fine or under-fine.

Health is good, — power, life, that resists disease, poison, and all enemies, and is conservative
as well as creative. Here is question, every spring,
whether to graft with wax, or whether with clay;
whether to whitewash, or to potash, or to prune; but
the one point is the thrifty tree. A good tree that
agrees with the soil will grow in spite of blight, or
bug, or pruning, or neglect, by night and by day, in
all weathers and all treatments. Vivacity, leader-
ship, must be had, and we are not allowed to be

nice in choosing. We must fetch the pump with dirty water, if clean cannot be had. If we will make bread, we must have contagion, yeast, empty-ings, or what not, to induce fermentation into the dough; as the torpid artist seeks inspiration at any cost, by virtue or by vice, by friend or by fiend, by prayer or by wine. And we have a certain instinct that where is great amount of life, though gross and peccant, it has its own checks and purifications, and will be found at last in harmony with moral laws.

We watch in children with pathetic interest the degree in which they possess recuperative force. When they are hurt by us, or by each other, or go to the bottom of the class, or miss the annual prizes, or are beaten in the game, — if they lose heart and remember the mischance in their cham-ber at home, they have a serious check. But if they have the buoyancy and resistance that pre-occupies them with new interest in the new mo-ment, — the wounds cicatrize and the fibre is the tougher for the hurt.

One comes to value this *plus* health when he sees that all difficulties vanish before it. A timid man, listening to the alarmists in Congress and in the newspapers, and observing the profligacy of party, — sectional interests urged with a fury which shuts its eyes to consequences, with a mind made

up to desperate extremities, ballot in one hand and
rifle in the other, — might easily believe that he
and his country have seen their best days, and he
hardens himself the best he can against the coming
ruin.   But after this has been foretold with equal
confidence fifty times, and government six per cents
have not declined a quarter of a mill, he discovers
that the enormous elements of strength which are
here in play make our politics unimportant.   Personal power, freedom, and the resources of nature
strain every faculty of every citizen.   We prosper
with such vigor that like thrifty trees, which grow
in spite of ice, lice, mice, and borers, so we do not
suffer from the profligate swarms that fatten on the
national treasury.   The huge animals nourish huge
parasites, and the rancor of the disease attests the
strength of the constitution.   The same energy in
the Greek *Demos* drew the remark that the evils
of popular government appear greater than they
are ; there is compensation for them in the spirit
and energy it awakens.   The rough-and-ready
style which belongs to a people of sailors, foresters,
farmers, and mechanics, has its advantages.   Power
educates the potentate.   As long as our people quote
English standards they dwarf their own proportions.   A Western lawyer of eminence said to me
he wished it were a penal offence to bring an English law-book into a court in this country, so perni-

cious had he found in his experience our deference
to English precedent. The very word ' commerce '
has only an English meaning, and is pinched to the
cramp exigencies of English experience. The commerce of rivers, the commerce of railroads, and who
knows but the commerce of air-balloons, must add
an American extension to the pond-hole of admiral-
ty. As long as our people quote English standards they will miss the sovereignty of power; but
let these rough riders — legislators in shirt-sleeves,
Hoosier, Sucker, Wolverine, Badger, or whatever
hard head Arkansas, Oregon, or Utah sends, half
orator, half assassin, to represent its wrath and
cupidity at Washington, — let these drive as they
may, and the disposition of territories and public
lands, the necessity of balancing and keeping at
bay the snarling majorities of German, Irish, and
of native millions, will bestow promptness, address,
and reason, at last, on our buffalo-hunter, and
authority and majesty of manners. The instinct
of the people is right. Men expect from good
whigs put into office by the respectability of the
country, much less skill to deal with Mexico,
Spain, Britain, or with our own malcontent members, than from some strong transgressor, like Jefferson or Jackson, who first conquers his own government and then uses the same genius to conquer
the foreigner. The senators who dissented from

Mr. Polk's Mexican war were not those who knew better, but those who from political position could afford it ; not Webster, but Benton and Calhoun.

This power to be sure is not clothed in satin. 'T is the power of Lynch law, of soldiers and pirates ; and it bullies the peaceable and loyal. But it brings its own antidote ; and here is my point, — that all kinds of power usually emerge at the same time ; good energy and bad ; power of mind with physical health ; the ecstasies of devotion with the exasperations of debauchery. The same elements are always present, only sometimes these conspicuous, and sometimes those ; what was yesterday foreground, being to-day background ; — what was surface, playing now a not less effective part as basis. The longer the drought lasts the more is the atmosphere surcharged with water. The faster the ball falls to the sun, the force to fly off is by so much augmented. And in morals, wild liberty breeds iron conscience ; natures with great impulses have great resources, and return from far. In politics, the sons of democrats will be whigs ; whilst red republicanism in the father is a spasm of nature to engender an intolerable tyrant in the next age. On the other hand, conservatism, ever more timorous and narrow, disgusts the children and drives them for a mouthful of fresh air into radicalism.

Those who have most of this coarse energy, — the 'bruisers,' who have run the gauntlet of caucus and tavern through the county or the state,— have their own vices, but they have the good-nature of strength and courage. Fierce and unscrupulous, they are usually frank and direct and above false-hood. Our politics fall into bad hands, and church-men and men of refinement, it seems agreed, are not fit persons to send to Congress. Politics is a deleterious profession, like some poisonous handi-crafts. Men in power have no opinions, but may be had cheap for any opinion, for any purpose; and if it be only a question between the most civil and the most forcible, I lean to the last. These Hoosiers and Suckers are really better than the snivelling opposition. Their wrath is at least of a bold and manly cast. They see, against the unan-imous declarations of the people, how much crime the people will bear; they proceed from step to step, and they have calculated but too justly upon their Excellencies the New England governors, and upon their Honors the New England legisla-tors. The messages of the governors and the res-olutions of the legislatures are a proverb for expressing a sham virtuous indignation, which, in the course of events, is sure to be belied.

In trade also this energy usually carries a trace of ferocity. Philanthropic and religious bodies do

not commonly make their executive officers out
of saints. The communities hitherto founded by
socialists, — the Jesuits, the Port-Royalists, the
American communities at New Harmony, at Brook
Farm, at Zoar, are only possible by installing Ju-
das as steward. The rest of the offices may be
filled by good burgesses. The pious and charitable
proprietor has a foreman not quite so pious and
charitable. The most amiable of country gentlemen has a certain pleasure in the teeth of the bull-
dog which guards his orchard. Of the Shaker society it was formerly a sort of proverb in the country that they always sent the devil to market. And
in representations of the Deity, painting, poetry,
and popular religion have ever drawn the wrath
from Hell. It is an esoteric doctrine of society
that a little wickedness is good to make muscle;
as if conscience were not good for hands and legs;
as if poor decayed formalists of law and order cannot run like wild goats, wolves, and conies; that
as there is a use in medicine for poisons, so the
world cannot move without rogues; that public
spirit and the ready hand are as well found among
the malignants. 'T is not very rare, the coincidence of sharp private and political practice with
public spirit and good neighborhood. I knew a
burly Boniface who for many years kept a public-
house in one of our rural capitals. He was a

knave whom the town could ill spare. He was a social, vascular creature, grasping and selfish. There was no crime which he did not or could not commit. But he made good friends of the select-men, served them with his best chop when they supped at his house, and also with his honor the Judge he was very cordial, grasping his hand. He introduced all the fiends, male and female, into the town, and united in his person the functions of bully, incendiary, swindler, barkeeper, and bur-glar. He girdled the trees and cut off the horses' tails of the temperance people, in the night. He led the 'rummies' and radicals in town-meeting with a speech. Meantime he was civil, fat, and easy, in his house, and precisely the most public-spirited citizen. He was active in getting the roads repaired and planted with shade-trees; he subscribed for the fountains, the gas, and the tele-graph; he introduced the new horse-rake, the new scraper, the baby-jumper, and what not, that Con-necticut sends to the admiring citizens. He did this the easier that the peddler stopped at his house, and paid his keeping by setting up his new trap on the landlord's premises.

Whilst thus the energy for originating and exe-cuting work deforms itself by excess, and so our axe chops off our own fingers, — this evil is not without remedy. All the elements whose aid man

calls in will sometimes become his masters, especially those of most subtle force. Shall he then
renounce steam, fire, and electricity, or shall he
learn to deal with them? The rule for this whole
class of agencies is, — all *plus* is good; only put it
in the right place.

Men of this surcharge of arterial blood cannot
live on nuts, herb-tea, and elegies; cannot read
novels and play whist; cannot satisfy all their
wants at the Thursday Lecture or the Boston
Athenæum. They pine for adventure, and must
go to Pike's Peak; had rather die by the hatchet
of a Pawnee than sit all day and every day at a
counting-room desk. They are made for war, for
the sea, for mining, hunting, and clearing; for
hair-breadth adventures, huge risks, and the joy of
eventful living. Some men cannot endure an hour
of calm at sea. I remember a poor Malay cook on
board a Liverpool packet, who, when the wind
blew a gale, could not contain his joy; "Blow!"
he cried, "me do tell you, blow!" Their friends
and governors must see that some vent for their
explosive complexion is provided. The roisters
who are destined for infamy at home, if sent to
Mexico will "cover you with glory," and come
back heroes and generals. There are Oregons,
Californias, and Exploring Expeditions enough
appertaining to America to find them in files to

gnaw and in crocodiles to eat. The young English
are fine animals, full of blood, and when they have
no wars to breathe their riotous valors in, they
seek for travels as dangerous as war, diving into
Maelstroms; swimming Hellesponts; wading up the
snowy Himmaleh; hunting lion, rhinoceros, elephant, in South Africa; gypsying with Borrow in
Spain and Algiers; riding alligators in South
America with Waterton; utilizing Bedouin, Sheik,
and Pacha, with Layard; yachting among the icebergs of Lancaster Sound; peeping into craters on
the equator; or running on the creases of Malays
in Borneo.

The excess of virility has the same importance
in general history as in private and industrial life.
Strong race or strong individual rests at last on
natural forces, which are best in the savage, who,
like the beasts around him, is still in reception of
the milk from the teats of Nature. Cut off the
connection between any of our works and this aboriginal source, and the work is shallow. The people lean on this, and the mob is not quite so bad
an argument as we sometimes say, for it has this
good side. "March without the people," said a
French deputy from the tribune, "and you march
into night: their instincts are a finger-pointing of
Providence, always turned toward real benefit.
But when you espouse an Orleans party, or a Bour-

bon or a Montalembert party, or any other but an
organic party, though you mean well, you have a
personality instead of a principle, which will inevitably drag you into a corner."

The best anecdotes of this force are to be had
from savage life, in explorers, soldiers, and bucca-
neers. But who cares for fallings-out of assassins
and fights of bears or grindings of icebergs ? Physical force has no value where there is nothing else.
Snow in snow-banks, fire in volcanoes and solfata-
ras is cheap. The luxury of ice is in tropical countries and midsummer days. The luxury of fire is
to have a little on our hearth; and of electricity,
not volleys of the charged cloud, but the manage-
able stream on the battery-wires. So of spirit, or
energy; the rests or remains of it in the civil and
moral man are worth all the cannibals in the Pacific.

In history the great moment is when the savage
is just ceasing to be a savage, with all his hairy
Pelasgic strength directed on his opening sense of
beauty : — and you have Pericles and Phidias, not
yet passed over into the Corinthian civility.
Everything good in nature and the world is in
that moment of transition, when the swarthy juices
still flow plentifully from nature, but their astrin-
gency or acridity is got out by ethics and humanity.

The triumphs of peace have been in some proximity to war. Whilst the hand was still familiar with the sword-hilt, whilst the habits of the camp were still visible in the port and complexion of the gentleman, his intellectual power culminated: the compression and tension of these stern conditions is a training for the finest and softest arts, and can rarely be compensated in tranquil times, except by some analogous vigor drawn from occupations as hardy as war.

We say that success is constitutional; depends on a *plus* condition of mind and body, on power of work, on courage; that it is of main efficacy in carrying on the world, and though rarely found in the right state for an article of commerce, but oftener in the supersaturate or excess which makes it dangerous and destructive, — yet it cannot be spared, and must be had in that form, and absorbents provided to take off its edge.

The affirmative class monopolize the homage of mankind. They originate and execute all the great feats. What a force was coiled up in the skull of Napoleon! Of the sixty thousand men making his army at Eylau, it seems some thirty thousand were thieves and burglars. The men whom in peaceful communities we hold if we can with iron at their legs, in prisons, under the muskets of sentinels, — this man dealt with hand to hand, dragged them to their duty, and won his victories by their bayonets.

This aboriginal might gives a surprising pleasure when it appears under conditions of supreme refinement, as in the proficients in high art. When Michel Angelo was forced to paint the Sistine Chapel in fresco, of which art he knew nothing, he went down into the Pope's gardens behind the Vatican, and with a shovel dug out ochres, red and yellow, mixed them with glue and water with his own hands, and having after many trials at last suited himself, climbed his ladders, and painted away, week after week, month after month, the sibyls and prophets. He surpassed his successors in rough vigor, as much as in purity of intellect and refinement. He was not crushed by his one picture left unfinished at last. Michel was wont to draw his figures first in skeleton, then to clothe them with flesh, and lastly to drape them. " Ah ! " said a brave painter to me, thinking on these things, "if a man has failed, you will find he has dreamed instead of working. There is no way to success in our art but to take off your coat, grind paint, and work like a digger on the railroad, all day and every day."

Success goes thus invariably with a certain *plus* or positive power: an ounce of power must balance an ounce of weight. And though a man cannot return into his mother's womb and be born with new amounts of vivacity, yet there are two economies which are the best *succedanea* which the case admits. The first is the stopping off decisively our miscellaneous activity and concentrating our force on one or a few points; as the gardener, by severe pruning, forces the sap of the tree into one or two vigorous limbs, instead of suffering it to spindle into a sheaf of twigs.

"Enlarge not thy destiny," said the oracle, "endeavor not to do more than is given thee in charge." The one prudence in life is concentration; the one evil is dissipation; and it makes no difference whether our dissipations are coarse or fine; property and its cares, friends and a social habit, or politics, or music, or feasting. Every thing is good which takes away one plaything and delusion more and drives us home to add one stroke of faithful work. Friends, books, pictures, lower duties, talents, flatteries, hopes, — all are distractions which cause oscillations in our giddy balloon, and make a good poise and a straight course impossible. You must elect your work; you shall take what your brain can, and drop all the rest. Only so can that amount of vital force accumulate which can make the step from knowing to doing. No matter how much faculty of idle seeing a man has, the step from knowing to doing is rarely taken.

'T is a step out of a chalk circle of imbecility into fruitfulness. Many an artist, lacking this, lacks all ; he sees the masculine Angelo or Cellini with despair. He too is up to Nature and the First Cause in his thought. But the spasm to collect and swing his whole being into one act, he has not. The poet Campbell said that " a man accustomed to work, was equal to any achievement he resolved on, and that for himself, necessity, not inspiration was the prompter of his muse."

Concentration is the secret of strength in politics, in war, in trade, in short in all management of human affairs. One of the high anecdotes of the world is the reply of Newton to the inquiry "how he had been able to achieve his discoveries?" — " By always intending my mind." Or if you will have a text from politics, take this from Plutarch ; " There was, in the whole city, but one street in which Pericles was ever seen, the street which led to the market-place and the council house. He declined all invitations to banquets, and all gay assemblies and company. During the whole period of his administration he never dined at the table of a friend." Or if we seek an example from trade, — " I hope," said a good man to Rothschild, "your children are not too fond of money and business; I am sure you would not wish that." — "I am sure I should wish that; I wish them to give mind, soul, heart, and body to business, — that is the way to be happy. It requires a great deal of boldness and a great deal of caution to make a great fortune, and when you have got it, it requires ten times as much wit to keep it. If I were to listen to all the projects proposed to me, I should ruin myself very soon. Stick to one business, young man. Stick to your brewery (he said this to young Buxton), and you will be the great brewer of London. Be brewer, and banker, and merchant, and manufacturer, and you will soon be in the Gazette."

Many men are knowing, many are apprehensive and tenacious, but they do not rush to a decision. But in our flowing affairs a decision must be made, — the best, if you can, but any is better than none. There are twenty ways of going to a point, and one is the shortest; but set out at once on one. A man who has that presence of mind which can bring to him on the instant all he knows, is worth for action a dozen men who know as much but can only bring it to light slowly. The good Speaker in the House is not the man who knows the theory of parliamentary tactics, but the man who decides off-hand. The good judge is not he who does hair-splitting justice to every allegation, but who, aiming at substantial justice, rules something intelligible for the guidance of suitors. The good lawyer is not the man who has an eye to every side and angle of contingency, and qualifies all his qualifications, but who throws himself on your part so heartily that he can get you out of a scrape. Dr. Johnson said, in one of his flowing sentences, "Miserable beyond all names of wretchedness is that unhappy pair, who are doomed to reduce beforehand to the principles of abstract reason all the details of each domestic day. There are cases where little can be said, and much must be done."

The second substitute for temperament is drill, the power of use and routine. The hack is a better roadster than the Arab barb. In chemistry, the galvanic stream, slow but continuous, is equal in power to the electric spark, and is, in our arts, a better agent. So in human action, against the spasm of energy we offset the continuity of drill. We spread the same amount of force over much time, instead of condensing it into a moment. 'T is the same ounce of gold here in a ball, and there in a leaf. At West Point, Col. Buford, the chief engineer, pounded with a hammer on the trunnions of a cannon until he broke them off. He fired a piece of ordnance some hundred times in swift succession, until it burst. Now which stroke broke the trunnion? Every stroke. Which blast burst the piece? Every blast. "*Diligence passe sens*," Henry VIII. was wont to say, or great is drill. John

Kemble said that the worst provincial company of actors would go through a play better than the best amateur company. Basil Hall likes to show that the worst regular troops will beat the best volunteers. Practice is nine tenths. A course of mobs is good practice for orators. All the great speakers were bad speakers at first. Stumping it through England for seven years made Cobden a consummate debater. Stumping it through New England for twice seven trained Wendell Phillips. The way to learn German is to read the same dozen pages over and over a hundred times, till you know every word and particle in them and can pronounce and repeat them by heart. No genius can recite a ballad at first reading so well as mediocrity can at the fifteenth or twentieth reading. The rule for hospitality and Irish 'help' is to have the same dinner every day throughout the year. At last, Mrs. O'Shaughnessy learns to cook it to a nicety, the host learns to carve it, and the guests are well served. A humorous friend of mine thinks that the reason why Nature is so perfect in her art, and gets up such inconceivably fine sunsets, is that she has learned how, at last, by dint of doing the same thing so very often. Cannot one converse better on a topic on which he has experience, than on one which is new? Men whose opinion is valued on 'Change are only such as have a special experience, and off that ground their opinion is not valuable. "More are made good by exercitation than by nature," said Democritus. The friction in nature is so enormous that we cannot spare any power. It is not question to express our thought, to elect our way, but to overcome resistances of the medium and material in everything we do. Hence the use of drill, and the worthlessness of amateurs to cope with practitioners. Six hours every day at the piano, only to give facility of touch; six hours a day at painting, only to give command of the odious materials, oil, ochres and brushes. The masters say that they know a master in music, only by seeing the pose of the hands on the keys; — so difficult and vital an act is the command of the instrument. To have learned the use of the tools, by thousands of manipulations; to have learned the arts of reckoning, by endless adding and dividing, is the power of the mechanic and the clerk.

I remarked in England, in confirmation of a frequent experience at home, that in literary circles, the men of trust and consideration, bookmakers, editors, university deans and professors, bishops too, were by no means men of the largest literary talent, but usually of a low and ordinary intellectuality, with a sort of mercantile activity and working talent. Indifferent hacks and mediocrities tower, by pushing their forces to a lucrative point or by working power, over multitudes of superior men, in Old as in New England.

I have not forgotten that there are sublime considerations which limit the value of talent and superficial success. We can easily overpraise the vulgar hero. There are sources on which we have not drawn. I know what I abstain from. I adjourn what I have to say on this topic to the chapters on Culture and Worship. But this force or spirit, being the means relied on by Nature for bringing the work of the day about, — as far as we attach importance to household life and the prizes of the world, we must respect that. And I hold that an economy may be applied to it; it is as much a subject of exact law and arithmetic as fluids and gases are; it may be husbanded or wasted; every man is efficient only as he is a container or vessel of this force, and never was any signal act or achievement in history but by this expenditure. This is not gold, but the gold-maker; not the fame, but the exploit.

If these forces and this husbandry are within reach of our will, and the laws of them can be read, we infer that all success and all conceivable benefit for man, is also, first or last, within his reach, and has its own sublime economies by which it may be attained. The world is mathematical, and has no casualty in all its vast and flowing curve. Success has no more eccentricity than the gingham and muslin we weave in our mills. I know no more affecting lesson to our busy, plotting New England brains, than to go into one of the factories with which we have lined all the watercourses in the States. A man hardly knows how much he is a machine until he begins to make telegraph, loom, press, and locomotive, in his own image. But in these he is forced to leave out his follies and hindrances, so that when we go to the mill, the machine is more moral than we. Let a man dare go to a loom and see if he be equal to it. Let machine confront machine, and see how they come out. The world-mill is more complex than the calico-mill, and the architect stooped less. In the gingham-mill, a broken thread or a shred spoils the web through a piece of a hundred yards, and is traced back to the girl that wove it, and lessens her wages. The stockholder, on being shown this, rubs his hands with delight. Are you so cunning, Mr. Profitloss, and do you expect to swindle *your* master and employer, in the web you weave? A day is a more magnificent cloth than any muslin, the mechanism that makes it is infinitely cunninger, and you shall not conceal the sleezy, fraudulent, rotten hours you have slipped into the piece; nor fear that any honest thread, or straighter steel, or more inflexible shaft, will not testify in the web.

III.

WEALTH.

—◆—

Who shall tell what did befall,
Far away in time, when once,
Over the lifeless ball,
Hung idle stars and suns?
What god the element obeyed?
Wings of what wind the lichen bore,
Wafting the puny seeds of power,
Which, lodged in rock, the rock abrade?
And well the primal pioneer
Knew the strong task to it assigned,
Patient through Heaven's enormous year
To build in matter home for mind.
From air the creeping centuries drew
The matted thicket low and wide,
This must the leaves of ages strew
The granite slab to clothe and hide,
Ere wheat can wave its golden pride.
What smiths, and in what furnace, rolled
(In dizzy æons dim and mute
The reeling brain can ill compute)
Copper and iron, lead, and gold?
What oldest star the fame can save

Of races perishing to pave
The planet with a floor of lime?
Dust is their pyramid and mole:
Who saw what ferns and palms were pressed
Under the tumbling mountain's breast,
In the safe herbal of the coal?
But when the quarried means were piled,
All is waste and worthless, till
Arrives the wise selecting will,
And, out of slime and chaos, Wit
Draws the threads of fair and fit.
Then temples rose, and towns, and marts,
The shop of toil, the hall of arts;
Then flew the sail across the seas
To feed the North from tropic trees;
The storm-wind wove, the torrent span,
Where they were bid the rivers ran;
New slaves fulfilled the poet's dream,
Galvanic wire, strong-shouldered steam.
Then docks were built, and crops were stored,
And ingots added to the hoard.
But, though light-headed man forget,
Remembering Matter pays her debt:
Still, through her motes and masses, draw
Electric thrills and ties of Law,
Which bind the strengths of Nature wild
To the conscience of a child.

WEALTH.

As soon as a stranger is introduced into any company, one of the first questions which all wish to have answered, is, How does that man get his living? And with reason. He is no whole man until he knows how to earn a blameless livelihood. Society is barbarous until every industrious man can get his living without dishonest customs.

Every man is a consumer, and ought to be a producer. He fails to make his place good in the world unless he not only pays his debt but also adds something to the common wealth. Nor can he do justice to his genius without making some larger demand on the world than a bare subsistence. He is by constitution expensive, and needs to be rich.

Wealth has its source in applications of the mind to nature, from the rudest strokes of spade and axe up to the last secrets of art. Intimate ties subsist between thought and all production; because a better order is equivalent to vast amounts of brute labor. The forces and the resistances are Nature's, but the mind acts in bringing things from where they abound to where they are wanted; in wise combining; in directing the practice of the useful arts, and in the creation of finer values by fine art, by eloquence, by song, or the reproductions of memory. Wealth is in applications of mind to nature; and the art of getting rich consists not in industry, much less in saving, but in a better order, in timeliness, in being at the right spot. One man has stronger arms or longer legs; another sees by the course of streams and growth of markets where land will be wanted, makes a clearing to the river, goes to sleep and wakes up rich. Steam is no stronger now than it was a hundred years ago; but is put to better use. A clever fellow was acquainted with the expansive force of steam; he also saw the wealth of wheat and grass rotting in Michigan. Then he cunningly screws on the steam-pipe to the wheat-crop. Puff now, O Steam! The steam puffs and expands as before, but this time it is dragging all Michigan at its back to hungry New York and hungry England. Coal lay in ledges under the ground since the Flood, until a laborer with pick and windlass brings it to the surface. We may well call it black diamonds. Every basket is power and civilization. For coal is a portable climate. It carries the heat of the tropics to Labrador and the polar circle; and it is the means of transporting itself whithersoever it is wanted. Watt and Stephenson whispered in the ear of mankind their secret, that *a half-ounce of coal will*

draw two tons a mile, and coal carries coal, by rail
and by boat, to make Canada as warm as Calcutta;
and with its comfort brings its industrial power.

When the farmer's peaches are taken from under the tree and carried into town, they have a new
look and a hundredfold value over the fruit which
grew on the same bough and lies fulsomely on the
ground. The craft of the merchant is this bringing a thing from where it abounds to where it is
costly.

Wealth begins in a tight roof that keeps the rain
and wind out; in a good pump that yields you
plenty of sweet water; in two suits of clothes, so to
change your dress when you are wet; in dry sticks
to burn, in a good double-wick lamp, and three
meals; in a horse or a locomotive to cross the land,
in a boat to cross the sea; in tools to work with,
in books to read; and so in giving on all sides by
tools and auxiliaries the greatest possible extension to our powers; as if it added feet and hands
and eyes and blood, length to the day, and knowledge and good-will.

Wealth begins with these articles of necessity.
And here we must recite the iron law which Nature thunders in these northern climates. First
she requires that each man should feed himself. If
happily his fathers have left him no inheritance, he
must go to work, and by making his wants less or

his gains more, he must draw himself out of that
state of pain and insult in which she forces the
beggar to lie. She gives him no rest until this is
done ; she starves, taunts, and torments him, takes
away warmth, laughter, sleep, friends, and day-
light, until he has fought his way to his own loaf.
Then, less peremptorily but still with sting enough,
she urges him to the acquisition of such things as
belong to him. Every warehouse and shop-win-
dow, every fruit-tree, every thought of every hour
opens a new want to him which it concerns his
power and dignity to gratify. It is of no use to
argue the wants down : the philosophers have laid
the greatness of man in making his wants few,
but will a man content himself with a hut and a
handful of dried pease ? He is born to be rich.
He is thoroughly related ; and is tempted out by
his appetites and fancies to the conquest of this
and that piece of nature, until he finds his well-
being in the use of his planet, and of more planets
than his own. Wealth requires, besides the crust
of bread and the roof, — the freedom of the city,
the freedom of the earth, travelling, machinery, the
benefits of science, music and fine arts, the best
culture and the best company. He is the rich man
who can avail himself of all men's faculties. He
is the richest man who knows how to draw a benefit from the labors of the greatest number of men,

of men in distant countries and in past times. The
same correspondence that is between thirst in the
stomach and water in the spring, exists between
the whole of man and the whole of nature. The
elements offer their service to him. The sea, wash-
ing the equator and the poles, offers its perilous
aid and the power and empire that follow it, —
day by day to his craft and audacity. " Beware of
me," it says, "but if you can hold me, I am the
key to all the lands." Fire offers, on its side,
an equal power. Fire, steam, lightning, gravity,
ledges of rock, mines of iron, lead, quicksilver, tin
and gold; forests of all woods; fruits of all climates ; animals of all habits; the powers of tillage;
the fabrics of his chemic laboratory; the webs of
his loom ; the masculine draught of his locomotive,
the talismans of the machine-shop; all grand and
subtile things, minerals, gases, ethers, passions,
war, trade, government, — are his natural play-
mates, and according to the excellence of the machinery in each human being is his attraction for
the instruments he is to employ. The world is his
tool-chest, and he is successful, or his education is
carried on just so far, as is the marriage of his faculties with nature, or the degree in which he takes
up things into himself.

The strong race is strong on these terms. The
Saxons are the merchants of the world ; now, for

a thousand years, the leading race, and by nothing more than their quality of personal independence, and in its special modification, pecuniary independence. No reliance for bread and games on the government; no clanship, no patriarchal style of living by the revenues of a chief, no marrying-on, no system of clientship suits them; but every man must pay his scot. The English are prosperous and peaceable, with their habit of considering that every man must take care of himself and has himself to thank if he do not maintain and improve his position in society.

The subject of economy mixes itself with morals, inasmuch as it is a peremptory point of virtue that a man's independence be secured. Poverty demoralizes. A man in debt is so far a slave, and Wall street thinks it easy for a *millionaire* to be a man of his word, a man of honor, but that in failing circumstances no man can be relied on to keep his integrity. And when one observes in the hotels and palaces of our Atlantic capitals the habit of expense, the riot of the senses, the absence of bonds, clanship, fellow-feeling of any kind, — he feels that when a man or a woman is driven to the wall, the chances of integrity are frightfully diminished; as if virtue were coming to be a luxury which few could afford, or, as Burke said, "at a market almost too high for humanity." He may fix his inventory of necessities and of enjoyments on what scale he pleases, but if he wishes the power and privilege of thought, the chalking out his own career and having society on his own terms, he must bring his wants within his proper power to satisfy.

The manly part is to do with might and main what you can do. The world is full of fops who never did anything and who have persuaded beauties and men of genius to wear their fop livery; and these will deliver the fop opinion, that it is not respectable to be seen earning a living; that it is much more respectable to spend without earning; and this doctrine of the snake will come also from the elect sons of light; for wise men are not wise at all hours, and will speak five times from their taste or their humor, to once from their reason. The brave workman, who might betray his feeling of it in his manners if he do not succumb in his practice, must replace the grace or elegance forfeited, by the merit of the work done. No matter whether he makes shoes, or statues, or laws. It is the privilege of any human work which is well done to invest the doer with a certain haughtiness. He can well afford not to conciliate, whose faithful work will answer for him. The mechanic at his bench carries a quiet heart and assured manners, and deals on even terms

with men of any condition. The artist has made
his picture so true that it disconcerts criticism.
The statue is so beautiful that it contracts no
stain from the market, but makes the market a
silent gallery for itself. The case of the young
lawyer was pitiful to disgust, — a paltry matter
of buttons or tweezer-cases ; but the determined
youth saw in it an aperture to insert his dangerous
wedges, made the insignificance of the thing forgotten, and gave fame by his sense and energy to
the name and affairs of the Tittleton snuff-box
factory.

Society in large towns is babyish, and wealth is
made a toy. The life of pleasure is so ostenta-
tious that a shallow observer must believe that
this is the agreed best use of wealth, and, whatever
is pretended, it ends in cosseting. But if this
were the main use of surplus capital, it would
bring us to barricades, burned towns and toma-
hawks, presently. Men of sense esteem wealth to
be the assimilation of nature to themselves, the
converting of the sap and juices of the planet to
the incarnation and nutriment of their design.
Power is what they want, not candy ; — power to
execute their design, power to give legs and feet,
form and actuality to their thought; which, to a
clear-sighted man, appears the end for which the
Universe exists, and all its resources might be well

applied. Columbus thinks that the sphere is a problem for practical navigation as well as for closet geometry, and looks on all kings and peoples as cowardly landsmen until they dare fit him out. Few men on the planet have more truly belonged to it. But he was forced to leave much of his map blank. His successors inherited his map, and inherited his fury to complete it.

So the men of the mine, telegraph, mill, map and survey, — the monomaniacs who talk up their project in marts and offices and entreat men to subscribe : — how did our factories get built? how did North America get netted with iron rails, except by the importunity of these orators who dragged all the prudent men in? Is party the madness of many for the gain of a few? This *speculative* genius is the madness of a few for the gain of the world. The projectors are sacrificed, but the public is the gainer. Each of these idealists, working after his thought, would make it tyrannical, if he could. He is met and antagonized by other speculators as hot as he. The equilibrium is preserved by these counteractions, as one tree keeps down another in the forest, that it may not absorb all the sap in the ground. And the supply in nature of railroad-presidents, copperminers, grand-junctioners, smoke-burners, fire-annihilators, &c., is limited by the same law which keeps the proportion in the supply of carbon, of alum, and of hydrogen.

To be rich is to have a ticket of admission to the master-works and chief men of each race. It is to have the sea, by voyaging; to visit the mountains, Niagara, the Nile, the desert, Rome, Paris, Constantinople; to see galleries, libraries, arsenals, manufactories. The reader of Humboldt's "Cosmos" follows the marches of a man whose eyes, ears, and mind are armed by all the science, arts, and implements which mankind have anywhere accumulated, and who is using these to add to the stock. So it is with Denon, Beckford, Belzoni, Wilkinson, Layard, Kane, Lepsius and Livingston. "The rich man," says Saadi, "is everywhere expected and at home." The rich take up something more of the world into man's life. They include the country as well as the town, the ocean-side, the White Hills, the Far West and the old European homesteads of man, in their notion of available material. The world is his who has money to go over it. He arrives at the sea-shore and a sumptuous ship has floored and carpeted for him the stormy Atlantic, and made it a luxurious hotel, amid the horrors of tempests. The Persians say "'T is the same to him who wears a shoe, as if the whole earth were covered with leather."

Kings are said to have long arms, but every

man should have long arms, and should pluck his
living, his instruments, his power and his knowing, from the sun, moon, and stars. Is not then
the demand to be rich legitimate? Yet I have
never seen a rich man. I have never seen a man
as rich as all men ought to be, or with an adequate
command of nature. The pulpit and the press
have many commonplaces denouncing the thirst
for wealth; but if men should take these moralists
at their word and leave off aiming to be rich, the
moralists would rush to rekindle at all hazards this
love of power in the people, lest civilization should
be undone. Men are urged by their ideas to acquire the command over nature. Ages derive a
culture from the wealth of Roman Cæsars, Leo
Tenths, magnificent Kings of France, Grand Dukes
of Tuscany, Dukes of Devonshire, Townleys, Ver-
nons and Peels, in England; or whatever great
proprietors. It is the interest of all men that
there should be Vaticans and Louvres full of noble works of art; British Museums, and French
Gardens of Plants, Philadelphia Academies of Natural History, Bodleian, Ambrosian, Royal, Con-
gressional Libraries. It is the interest of all that
there should be Exploring Expeditions; Captain
Cooks to voyage round the world, Rosses, Franklins, Richardsons and Kanes, to find the magnetic
and the geographic poles. We are all richer for

the measurement of a degree of latitude on the
earth's surface.   Our navigation is safer for the
chart.   How intimately our knowledge of the system of the Universe rests on that! — and a true
economy in a state or an individual will forget its
frugality in behalf of claims like these.

Whilst it is each man's interest that not only
ease and convenience of living, but also wealth or
surplus product should exist somewhere, it need not
be in his hands.   Often it is very undesirable to
him.   Goethe said well, "Nobody should be rich
but those who understand it."   Some men are born
to own, and can animate all their possessions.
Others cannot: their owning is not graceful; seems
to be a compromise of their character; they seem
to steal their own dividends.   They should own
who can administer, not they who hoard and conceal; not they who, the greater proprietors they
are, are only the greater beggars, but they whose
work carves out work for more, opens a path for
all.   For he is the rich man in whom the people
are rich, and he is the poor man in whom the people are poor; and how to give all access to the
masterpieces of art and nature, is the problem of
civilization.   The socialism of our day has done
good service in setting men on thinking how certain civilizing benefits, now only enjoyed by the op-
ulent, can be enjoyed by all.   For example, the

providing to each man the means and apparatus of science and of the arts. There are many articles good for occasional use, which few men are able to own. Every man wishes to see the ring of Saturn, the satellites and belts of Jupiter and Mars, the mountains and craters in the moon ; yet how few can buy a telescope ! and of those, scarcely one would like the trouble of keeping it in order and exhibiting it. So of electrical and chemical apparatus, and many the like things. Every man may have occasion to consult books which he does not care to possess, such as cyclopedias, dictionaries, tables, charts, maps, and public documents ; pictures also of birds, beasts, fishes, shells, trees, flowers, whose names he desires to know.

There is a refining influence from the arts of Design on a prepared mind which is as positive as that of music, and not to be supplied from any other source. But pictures, engravings, statues and casts, beside their first cost, entail expenses, as of galleries and keepers for the exhibition ; and the use which any man can make of them is rare, and their value too is much enhanced by the numbers of men who can share their enjoyment. In the Greek cities it was reckoned profane that any person should pretend a property in a work of art, which belonged to all who could behold it. I think sometimes, could I only have music on my own terms; could I live in a great city and know where I could go whenever I wished the ablution and inundation of musical waves, — that were a bath and a medicine.

If properties of this kind were owned by states, towns, and lyceums, they would draw the bonds of neighborhood closer. A town would exist to an intellectual purpose. In Europe, where the feudal forms secure the permanence of wealth in certain families, those families buy and preserve these things and lay them open to the public. But in America, where democratic institutions divide every estate into small portions after a few years, the public should step into the place of these proprietors, and provide this culture and inspiration for the citizen.

Man was born to be rich, or inevitably grows rich by the use of his faculties; by the union of thought with nature. Property is an intellectual production. The game requires coolness, right reasoning, promptness and patience in the players. Cultivated labor drives out brute labor. An infinite number of shrewd men, in infinite years, have arrived at certain best and shortest ways of doing, and this accumulated skill in arts, cultures, harvestings, curings, manufactures, navigations, exchanges, constitutes the worth of our world to-day.

Commerce is a game of skill, which every man

cannot play, which few men can play well. The
right merchant is one who has the just average of
faculties we call *common-sense ;* a man of a strong
affinity for facts, who makes up his decision on
what he has seen. He is thoroughly persuaded of
the truths of arithmetic. There is always a reason,
in the man, for his good or bad fortune, and so in
making money. Men talk as if there were some
magic about this, and believe in magic, in all parts
of life. He knows that all goes on the old road,
pound for pound, cent for cent, — for every effect
a perfect cause, — and that good luck is another
name for tenacity of purpose. He insures himself
in every transaction, and likes small and sure gains.
Probity and closeness to the facts are the basis, but
the masters of the art add a certain long arithmetic. The problem is to combine many and remote
operations with the accuracy and adherence to the
facts which is easy in near and small transactions ;
so to arrive at gigantic results, without any compromise of safety. Napoleon was fond of telling
the story of the Marseilles banker who said to his
visitor, surprised at the contrast between the splendor of the banker's château and hospitality and the
meanness of the counting-room in which he had
seen him, — " Young man, you are too young to
understand how masses are formed ; the true and
only power, whether composed of money, water, or

men ; it is all alike ; a mass is an immense centre of motion, but it must be begun, it must be kept
up : " — and he might have added that the way in
which it must be begun and kept up is by obedience to the law of particles.

Success consists in close appliance to the laws of
the world, and since those laws are intellectual and
moral, an intellectual and moral obedience. Political Economy is as good a book wherein to read
the life of man and the ascendency of laws over all
private and hostile influences, as any Bible which
has come down to us.

Money is representative, and follows the nature
and fortunes of the owner. The coin is a delicate
meter of civil, social, and moral changes. The
farmer is covetous of his dollar, and with reason.
It is no waif to him. He knows how many strokes
of labor it represents. His bones ache with the
days' work that earned it. He knows how much
land it represents ; — how much rain, frost, and
sunshine. He knows that in the dollar he gives
you so much discretion and patience, so much hoe-
ing and threshing. Try to lift his dollar ; you
must lift all that weight. In the city, where money
follows the skit of a pen or a lucky rise in exchange, it comes to be looked on as light. I wish
the farmer held it dearer, and would spend it only
for real bread ; force for force.

The farmer's dollar is heavy and the clerk's is light and nimble; leaps out of his pocket; jumps on to cards and faro-tables : but still more curious is its susceptibility to metaphysical changes. It is the finest barometer of social storms, and announces revolutions.

Every step of civil advancement makes every man's dollar worth more. In California, the country where it grew, — what would it buy? A few years since, it would buy a shanty, dysentery, hunger, bad company and crime. There are wide countries, like Siberia, where it would buy little else to-day than some petty mitigation of suffering. In Rome it will buy beauty and magnificence. Forty years ago, a dollar would not buy much in Boston. Now it will buy a great deal more in our old town, thanks to railroads, telegraphs, steamers, and the contemporaneous growth of New York and the whole country. Yet there are many goods appertaining to a capital city which are not yet purchasable here, no, not with a mountain of dollars. A dollar in Florida is not worth a dollar in Massachusetts. A dollar is not value, but representative of value, and, at last, of moral values. A dollar is rated for the corn it will buy, or to speak strictly, not for the corn or house-room, but for Athenian corn, and Roman house-room, — for the wit, probity, and power which we eat bread and

dwell in houses to share and exert. Wealth is
mental; wealth is moral. The value of a dollar is,
to buy just things; a dollar goes on increasing in
value with all the genius and all the virtue of the
world. A dollar in a university is worth more
than a dollar in a jail; in a temperate, schooled,
law-abiding community than in some sink of crime,
where dice, knives and arsenic are in constant play.

The "Bank-Note Detector" is a useful publica-
tion. But the current dollar, silver or paper, is
itself the detector of the right and wrong where it
circulates. Is it not instantly enhanced by the increase of equity? If a trader refuses to sell his
vote, or adheres to some odious right, he makes so
much more equity in Massachusetts; and every
acre in the state is more worth, in the hour of his
action. If you take out of State Street the ten
honestest merchants and put in ten roguish persons
controlling the same amount of capital, the rates
of insurance will indicate it; the soundness of
banks will show it; the highways will be less secure; the schools will feel it, the children will
bring home their little dose of the poison; the
judge will sit less firmly on the bench, and his de-
cisions be less upright; he has lost so much support and constraint, which all need; and the pulpit will betray it, in a laxer rule of life. An apple-
tree, if you take out every day for a number of

days a load of loam and put in a load of sand about
its roots, will find it out. An apple-tree is a stupid kind of creature, but if this treatment be pur-
sued for a short time I think it would begin to mis-
trust something. And if you should take out of
the powerful class engaged in trade a hundred good
men and put in a hundred bad, or, what is just the
same thing, introduce a demoralizing institution,
would not the dollar, which is not much stupider
than an apple tree, presently find it out ? The
value of a dollar is social, as it is created by society. Every man who removes into this city with
any purchasable talent or skill in him, gives to
every man's labor in the city a new worth. If a
talent is anywhere born into the world, the community of nations is enriched ; and much more with a
new degree of probity. The expense of crime, one
of the principal charges of every nation, is so far
stopped. In Europe, crime is observed to increase
or abate with the price of bread. If the Roths-
childs at Paris do not accept bills, the people at
Manchester, at Paisley, at Birmingham are forced
into the highway, and landlords are shot down in
Ireland. The police-records attest it. The vibra-
tions are presently felt in New York, New Orleans,
and Chicago. Not much otherwise the economical
power touches the masses through the political
lords. Rothschild refuses the Russian loan, and

there is peace and the harvests are saved. He takes it, and there is war and an agitation through a large portion of mankind, with every hideous result, ending in revolution and a new order.

Wealth brings with it its own checks and balances. The basis of political economy is non-interference. The only safe rule is found in the self-adjusting meter of demand and supply. Do not legislate. Meddle, and you snap the sinews with your sumptuary laws. Give no bounties, make equal laws, secure life and property, and you need not give alms. Open the doors of opportunity to talent and virtue and they will do themselves justice, and property will not be in bad hands. In a free and just commonwealth, property rushes from the idle and imbecile to the industrious, brave and persevering.

The laws of nature play through trade, as a toy-battery exhibits the effects of electricity. The level of the sea is not more surely kept than is the equilibrium of value in society by the demand and supply; and artifice or legislation punishes itself by reactions, gluts, and bankruptcies. The sublime laws play indifferently through atoms and galaxies. Whoever knows what happens in the getting and spending of a loaf of bread and a pint of beer, that no wishing will change the rigorous limits of pints and penny loaves; that, for all that is consumed so much less remains in the basket and pot, but what is gone out of these is not wasted but well spent if it nourish his body and enable him to finish his task ; — knows all of political economy that the budgets of empires can teach him. The interest of petty economy is this symbolization of the great economy ; the way in which a house and a private man's methods tally with the solar system and the laws of give and take, throughout nature ; and however wary we are of the falsehoods and petty tricks which we suicidally play off on each other, every man has a certain satisfaction whenever his dealing touches on the inevitable facts ; when he sees that things themselves dictate the price, as they always tend to do, and, in large manufactures, are seen to do. Your paper is not fine or coarse enough, — is too heavy, or too thin. The manufacturer says he will furnish you with just that thickness or thinness you want ; the pattern is quite indifferent to him ; here is his schedule ; — any variety of paper, as cheaper or dearer, with the prices annexed. A pound of paper costs so much, and you may have it made up in any pattern you fancy.

There is in all our dealings a self-regulation that supersedes chaffering. You will rent a house, but must have it cheap. The owner can reduce the rent, but so he incapacitates himself from making proper repairs, and the tenant gets not the house he

would have, but a worse one; besides that a relation a little injurious is established between landlord and tenant. You dismiss your laborer, saying,
" Patrick, I shall send for you as soon as I cannot
do without you." Patrick goes off contented, for
he knows that the weeds will grow with the pota-
toes, the vines must be planted, next week, and
however unwilling you may be, the cantelopes,
crook-necks and cucumbers will send for him. Who
but must wish that all labor and value should stand
on the same simple and surly market? If it is the
best of its kind, it will. We must have joiner,
locksmith, planter, priest, poet, doctor, cook, weaver,
ostler; each in turn, through the year.

If a St. Michael's pear sells for a shilling, it costs
a shilling to raise it. If, in Boston, the best securi-
ties offer twelve per cent. for money, they have just
six per cent of insecurity. You may not see that the
fine pear costs you a shilling, but it costs the community so much. The shilling represents the number of enemies the pear has, and the amount of risk
in ripening it. The price of coal shows the narrow-
ness of the coal-field, and a compulsory confinement
of the miners to a certain district. All salaries
are reckoned on contingent as well as on actual
services. " If the wind were always southwest by
west," said the skipper, " women might take ships
to sea." One might say that all things are of one

price ; that nothing is cheap or dear, and that the
apparent disparities that strike us are only a shop-
man's trick of concealing the damage in your bargain. A youth coming into the city from his native New Hampshire farm, with its hard fare still
fresh in his remembrance, boards at a first-class
hotel, and believes he must somehow have out-
witted Dr. Franklin and Malthus, for luxuries are
cheap. But he pays for the one convenience of a
better dinner, by the loss of some of the richest social and educational advantages. He has lost what
guards! what incentives! He will perhaps find
by and by that he left the Muses at the door of the
hotel, and found the Furies inside. Money often
costs too much, and power and pleasure are not
cheap. The ancient poet said " The gods sell all
things at a fair price."

There is an example of the compensations in the
commercial history of this country. When the
European wars threw the carrying-trade of the
world, from 1800 to 1812, into American bottoms,
a seizure was now and then made of an American
ship. Of course the loss was serious to the owner,
but the country was indemnified ; for we charged
threepence a pound for carrying cotton, sixpence
for tobacco, and so on ; which paid for the risk and
loss, and brought into the country an immense prosperity, early marriages, private wealth, the building

of cities and of states: and after the war was over, we received compensation over and above, by treaty, for all the seizures. Well, the Americans grew rich and great. But the pay-day comes round. Britain, France, and Germany, which our extraordinary profits had impoverished, send out, attracted by the fame of our advantages, first their thousands then their millions of poor people, to share the crop. At first we employ them, and increase our prosperity; but, in the artificial system of society and of protected labor, which we also have adopted and enlarged, there come presently checks and stoppages. Then we refuse to employ these poor men. But they will not so be answered. They go into the poor-rates, and though we refuse wages, we must now pay the same amount in the form of taxes. Again, it turns out that the largest proportion of crimes are committed by foreigners. The cost of the crime and the expense of courts and of prisons we must bear, and the standing army of preventive police we must pay. The cost of education of the posterity of this great colony, I will not compute. But the gross amount of these costs will begin to pay back what we thought was a net gain from our transatlantic customers of 1800. It is vain to refuse this payment. We cannot get rid of these people, and we cannot get rid of their will to be supported. That has become an inevitable element of our politics; and, for their votes, each of the dominant parties courts and assists them to get it executed. Moreover, we have to pay, not what would have contented them at home, but what they have learned to think necessary here; so that opinion, fancy, and all manner of moral considerations complicate the problem.

There are few measures of economy which will bear to be named without disgust; for the subject is tender and we may easily have too much of it, and therein resembles the hideous animalcules of which our bodies are built up, — which, offensive in the particular, yet compose valuable and effective masses. Our nature and genius force us to respect ends, whilst we use means. We must use the means, and yet, in our most accurate using somehow screen and cloak them, as we can only give them any beauty by a reflection of the glory of the end. That is the good head, which serves the end and commands the means. The rabble are corrupted by their means; the means are too strong for them, and they desert their end.

1. The first of these measures is that each man's expense must proceed from his character. As long as your genius buys, the investment is safe, though you spend like a monarch. Nature arms each man with some faculty which enables him to do easily

some feat impossible to any other, and thus makes
him necessary to society. This native determination guides his labor and his spending. He wants
an equipment of means and tools proper to his talent. And to save on this point were to neutralize
the special strength and helpfulness of each mind.
Do your work, respecting the excellence of the
work, and not its acceptableness. This is so much
economy that, rightly read, it is the sum of economy. Profligacy consists not in spending years of
time or chests of money, — but in spending them
off the line of your career. The crime which bank-
rupts men and states is job-work; — declining from
your main design, to serve a turn here or there.
Nothing is beneath you, if it is in the direction of
your life; nothing is great or desirable if it is off
from that. I think we are entitled here to draw a
straight line and say that society can never prosper
but must always be bankrupt, until every man does
that which he was created to do.

Spend for your expense, and retrench the expense
which is not yours. Allston the painter was wont
to say that he built a plain house, and filled it with
plain furniture, because he would hold out no bribe
to any to visit him who had not similar tastes to
his own. We are sympathetic, and, like children,
want everything we see. But it is a large stride to
independence, when a man, in the discovery of

his proper talent, has sunk the necessity for false expenses. As the betrothed maiden by one secure affection is relieved from a system of slaveries, — the daily inculcated necessity of pleasing all, — so the man who has found what he can do, can spend on that and leave all other spending. Montaigne said, " When he was a younger brother, he went brave in dress and equipage, but afterward his château and farms might answer for him." Let a man who belongs to the class of nobles, those namely who have found out that they can do something, relieve himself of all vague squandering on objects not his. Let the realist not mind appearances. Let him delegate to others the costly courtesies and decorations of social life. The virtues are economists, but some of the vices are also. Thus, next to humility, I have noticed that pride is a pretty good husband. A good pride is, as I reckon it, worth from five hundred to fifteen hundred a year. Pride is handsome, economical ; pride eradicates so many vices, letting none subsist but itself, that it seems as if it were a great gain to exchange vanity for pride. Pride can go without domestics, without fine clothes, can live in a house with two rooms, can eat potato, purslain, beans, lyed corn, can work on the soil, can travel afoot, can talk with poor men, or sit silent well-contented in fine saloons. But vanity costs money, labor, horses, men, women, health, and peace, and is still nothing at last; a long way leading nowhere. Only one drawback; proud people are intolerably selfish, and the vain are gentle and giving.

Art is a jealous mistress, and if a man have a genius for painting, poetry, music, architecture, or philosophy, he makes a bad husband and an ill provider, and should be wise in season and not fetter himself with duties which will embitter his days and spoil him for his proper work. We had in this region, twenty years ago, among our educated men, a sort of Arcadian fanaticism, a passionate desire to go upon the land and unite farming to intellectual pursuits. Many effected their purpose and made the experiment, and some became downright ploughmen; but all were cured of their faith that scholarship and practical farming (I mean, with one's own hands) could be united.

With brow bent, with firm intent, the pale scholar leaves his desk to draw a freer breath and get a juster statement of his thought, in the garden-walk. He stoops to pull up a purslain or a dock that is choking the young corn, and finds there are two; close behind the last is a third; he reaches out his hand to a fourth, behind that are four thousand and one. He is heated and untuned, and by and by wakes up from his idiot dream of chickweed and red-root, to remember his morning thought, and to find that with his adamantine purposes he has been duped by a dandelion. A garden is like those pernicious machineries we read of every month in the newspapers, which catch a man's coat-skirt or his hand and draw in his arm, his leg and his whole body to irresistible destruction. In an evil hour he pulled down his wall and added a field to his homestead. No land is bad, but land is worse. If a man own land, the land owns him. Now let him leave home, if he dare. Every tree and graft, every hill of melons, row of corn, or quickset hedge; all he has done and all he means to do, stand in his way like duns, when he would go out of his gate. The devotion to these vines and trees he finds poisonous. Long free walks, a circuit of miles, free his brain and serve his body. Long marches are no hardship to him. He believes he composes easily on the hills. But this pottering in a few square yards of garden is dispiriting and drivelling. The smell of the plants has drugged him and robbed him of energy. He finds a catalepsy in his bones. He grows peevish and poor-spirited. The genius of reading and of gardening are antagonistic, like resinous and vitreous electricity. One is concentrative in sparks and shocks; the other is diffuse strength; so that each disqualifies its workman for the other's duties.

An engraver, whose hands must be of an exqui-

site delicacy of stroke, should not lay stone walls.
Sir David Brewster gives exact instructions for
microscopic observation: "Lie down on your back,
and hold the single lens and object over your eye,"
&c. &c. How much more the seeker of abstract
truth, who needs periods of isolation and rapt concentration and almost a going out of the body to
think !

2. Spend after your genius, *and by system*. Nature goes by rule, not by sallies and saltations.
There must be system in the economies. Saving
and unexpensiveness will not keep the most pathetic
family from ruin, nor will bigger incomes make free
spending safe. The secret of success lies never
in the amount of money, but in the relation of income to outgo; as, after expense has been fixed at
a certain point, then new and steady rills of income
though never so small being added, wealth begins.
But in ordinary, as means increase, spending increases faster, so that large incomes, in England
and elsewhere, are found not to help matters; —
the eating quality of debt does not relax its vorac-
ity. When the cholera is in the potato, what is the
use of planting larger crops? In England, the
richest country in the universe, I was assured by
shrewd observers that great lords and ladies had no
more guineas to give away than other people; that
liberality with money is as rare and as immediately

famous a virtue as it is here. Want is a growing
giant whom the coat of Have was never large
enough to cover. I remember in Warwickshire to
have been shown a fair manor, still in the same
name as in Shakspeare's time. The rent-roll I was
told is some fourteen thousand pounds a year; but
when the second son of the late proprietor was
born, the father was perplexed how to provide for
him. The eldest son must inherit the manor; what
to do with this supernumerary? He was advised
to breed him for the Church and to settle him in
the rectorship which was in the gift of the family;
which was done. It is a general rule in that country that bigger incomes do not help anybody. It
is commonly observed that a sudden wealth, like a
prize drawn in a lottery or a large bequest to a
poor family, does not permanently enrich. They
have served no apprenticeship to wealth, and with
the rapid wealth come rapid claims which they do
not know how to deny, and the treasure is quickly
dissipated.

A system must be in every economy, or the best
single expedients are of no avail. A farm is a
good thing when it begins and ends with itself,
and does not need a salary or a shop to eke it out.
Thus, the cattle are a main link in the chain-ring.
If the non-conformist or æsthetic farmer leaves out
the cattle and does not also leave out the want

which the cattle must supply, he must fill the gap
by begging or stealing.   When men now alive
were born, the farm yielded everything that was
consumed on it.   The farm yielded no money, and
the farmer got on without.   If he fell sick, his
neighbors came in to his aid; each gave a day's
work, or a half day; or lent his yoke of oxen, or
his horse, and kept his work even; hoed his pota-
toes, mowed his hay, reaped his rye; well knowing
that no man could afford to hire labor without sell-
ing his land.   In autumn a farmer could sell an ox
or a hog and get a little money to pay taxes withal.
Now, the farmer buys almost all he consumes, —
tin-ware, cloth, sugar, tea, coffee, fish, coal, railroad-
tickets and newspapers.

A master in each art is required, because the
practice is never with still or dead subjects, but
they change in your hands.   You think farm-build-
ings and broad acres a solid property; but its value
is flowing like water.   It requires as much watching as if you were decanting wine from a cask.
The farmer knows what to do with it, stops every
leak, turns all the streamlets to one reservoir and
decants wine ; but a blunderhead comes out of
Cornhill, tries his hand, and it all leaks away.   So
is it with granite streets or timber townships as
with fruit or flowers.   Nor is any investment so
permanent that it can be allowed to remain with-

out incessant watching, as the history of each attempt to lock up an inheritance through two generations for an unborn inheritor may show.

When Mr. Cockayne takes a cottage in the country, and will keep his cow, he thinks a cow is a creature that is fed on hay and gives a pail of milk twice a day. But the cow that he buys gives milk for three months; then her bag dries up. What to do with a dry cow? who will buy her? Perhaps he bought also a yoke of oxen to do his work; but they get blown and lame. What to do with blown and lame oxen? The farmer fats his after the spring-work is done, and kills them in the fall. But how can Cockayne, who has no pastures, and leaves his cottage daily in the cars at business hours, be pothered with fatting and killing oxen? He plants trees; but there must be crops, to keep the trees in ploughed land. What shall be the crops? He will have nothing to do with trees, but will have grass. After a year or two the grass must be turned up and ploughed; now what crops? Credulous Cockayne!

3. Help comes in the custom of the country, and the rule of *Impera parendo*. The rule is not to dictate nor to insist on carrying out each of your schemes by ignorant wilfulness, but to learn practically the secret spoken from all nature, that things themselves refuse to be mismanaged, and will show

to the watchful their own law. Nobody need stir
hand or foot. The custom of the country will do
it all. I know not how to build or to plant ; neither how to buy wood, nor what to do with the
house-lot, the field, or the wood-lot, when bought.
Never fear ; it is all settled how it shall be, long
beforehand, in the custom of the country, — whether
to sand or whether to clay it, when to plough, and
how to dress, whether to grass or to corn ; and you
cannot help or hinder it. Nature has her own best
mode of doing each thing, and she has somewhere
told it plainly, if we will keep our eyes and ears
open. If not, she will not be slow in undeceiving
us when we prefer our own way to hers. How
often we must remember the art of the surgeon,
which, in replacing the broken bone, contents itself
with releasing the parts from false position ; they
fly into place by the action of the muscles. On
this art of nature all our arts rely.

Of the two eminent engineers in the recent con-
struction of railways in England, Mr. Brunel went
straight from terminus to terminus, through mountains, over streams, crossing highways, cutting du-
cal estates in two, and shooting through this man's
cellar and that man's attic window, and so arriving
at his end, at great pleasure to geometers, but with
cost to his company. Mr. Stephenson on the contrary, believing that the river knows the way, fol-

lowed his valley as implicitly as our Western Rail-road follows the Westfield River, and turned out to be the safest and cheapest engineer. We say the cows laid out Boston. Well, there are worse surveyors. Every pedestrian in our pastures has frequent occasion to thank the cows for cutting the best path through the thicket and over the hills; and travellers and Indians know the value of a buffalo-trail, which is sure to be the easiest possible pass through the ridge.

When a citizen fresh from Dock Square or Milk Street comes out and buys land in the country, his first thought is to a fine outlook from his windows; his library must command a western view; a sunset every day, bathing the shoulder of Blue Hills, Wachusett, and the peaks of Monadnoc and Uncanoonuc. What, thirty acres, and all this magnificence for fifteen hundred dollars! It would be cheap at fifty thousand. He proceeds at once, his eyes dim with tears of joy, to fix the spot for his corner-stone. But the man who is to level the ground thinks it will take many hundred loads of gravel to fill the hollow to the road. The stonemason who should build the well thinks he shall have to dig forty feet; the baker doubts he shall never like to drive up to the door; the practical neighbor cavils at the position of the barn; and the citizen comes to know that his predecessor the

farmer built the house in the right spot for the sun
and wind, the spring, and water-drainage, and the
convenience to the pasture, the garden, the field
and the road.   So Dock Square yields the point,
and things have their own way.   Use has made the
farmer wise, and the foolish citizen learns to take
his counsel.   From step to step he comes at last to
surrender at discretion.   The farmer affects to take
his orders ; but the citizen says, You may ask me
as often as you will, and in what ingenious forms,
for an opinion concerning the mode of building my
wall, or sinking my well, or laying out my acre,
but the ball will rebound to you.   These are matters on which I neither know nor need to know
anything.   These are questions which you and not
I shall answer.

Not less within doors a system settles itself paramount and tyrannical over master and mistress,
servant and child, cousin and acquaintance.   'T is
in vain that genius or virtue or energy of character strive and cry against it.   This is fate.   And
't is very well that the poor husband reads in a
book of a new way of living, and resolves to adopt
it at home ; let him go home and try it, if he dare.

4.   Another point of economy is to look for
seed of the same kind as you sow, and not to hope
to buy one kind with another kind.   Friendship
buys friendship ; justice, justice ; military merit,

military success. Good husbandry finds wife, children and household. The good merchant, large gains, ships, stocks, and money. The good poet, fame and literary credit; but not either, the other. Yet there is commonly a confusion of expectations on these points. Hotspur lives for the moment, praises himself for it, and despises Furlong, that he does not. Hotspur of course is poor, and Furlong a good provider. The odd circumstance is that Hotspur thinks it a superiority in himself, this improvidence, which ought to be rewarded with Furlong's lands.

I have not at all completed my design. But we must not leave the topic without casting one glance into the interior recesses. It is a doctrine of philosophy that man is a being of degrees; that there is nothing in the world which is not repeated in his body, his body being a sort of miniature or summary of the world; then that there is nothing in his body which is not repeated as in a celestial sphere in his mind; then, there is nothing in his brain which is not repeated in a higher sphere in his moral system.

5. Now these things are so in Nature. All things ascend, and the royal rule of economy is that it should ascend also, or, whatever we do must always have a higher aim. Thus it is a maxim that money is another kind of blood. *Pe-*

cunia alter sanguis : or, the estate of a man is only a larger kind of body, and admits of regimen analogous to his bodily circulations. So there is no maxim of the merchant which does not admit of an extended sense, *e. g.*, " Best use of money is to pay debts ; " " Every business by itself ; " " Best time is present time ; " " The right investment is in tools of your trade ; " and the like. The counting-room maxims liberally expounded are laws of the Universe. The merchant's economy is a coarse symbol of the soul's economy. It is to spend for power and not for pleasure. It is to invest income ; that is to say to take up particulars into generals ; days into integral eras — literary, emotive, practical — of its life, and still to ascend in its investment. The merchant has but one rule, *absorb and invest ;* he is to be capitalist ; the scraps and filings must be gathered back into the crucible ; the gas and smoke must be burned, and earnings must not go to increase expense, but to capital again. Well, the man must be capitalist. Will he spend his income, or will he invest ? His body and every organ is under the same law. His body is a jar in which the liquor of life is stored. Will he spend for pleasure ? The way to ruin is short and facile. Will he not spend but hoard for power ? It passes through the sacred fermentations, by that law of Nature whereby everything climbs to higher platforms, and bodily vigor becomes mental and moral vigor. The bread he eats is first strength and animal spirits; it becomes, in higher laboratories, imagery and thought; and in still higher results, courage and endurance. This is the right compound interest; this is capital doubled, quadrupled, centupled; man raised to his highest power.

The true thrift is always to spend on the higher plane; to invest and invest, with keener avarice, that he may spend in spiritual creation and not in augmenting animal existence. Nor is the man enriched, in repeating the old experiments of animal sensation; nor unless through new powers and ascending pleasures he knows himself by the actual experience of higher good to be already on the way to the highest.

IV.

CULTURE.

———◆———

Can rules or tutors educate
The semigod whom we await?
He must be musical,
Tremulous, impressional,
Alive to gentle influence
Of landscape and of sky,
And tender to the spirit-touch
Of man's or maiden's eye :
But, to his native centre fast,
Shall into Future fuse the Past,
And the world's flowing fates in his own mould
    recast.

CULTURE.

THE word of ambition at the present day is Culture. Whilst all the world is in pursuit of power, and of wealth as a means of power, culture corrects the theory of success. A man is the prisoner of his power. A topical memory makes him an almanac; a talent for debate, a disputant; skill to get money makes him a miser, that is, a beggar. Culture reduces these inflammations by invoking the aid of other powers against the dominant talent, and by appealing to the rank of powers. It watches success. For performance, Nature has no mercy, and sacrifices the performer to get it done; makes a dropsy or a tympany of him. If she wants a thumb, she makes one at the cost of arms and legs, and any excess of power in one part is usually paid for at once by some defect in a contiguous part.

Our efficiency depends so much on our concentration, that Nature usually in the instances where a marked man is sent into the world, overloads him with bias, sacrificing his symmetry to his working power. It is said a man can write but one book; and if a man have a defect, it is apt to leave its impression on all his performances. If she creates a

policeman like Fouché, he is made up of suspicions
and of plots to circumvent them. "The air," said
Fouché, "is full of poniards." The physician
Sanctorius spent his life in a pair of scales, weigh-
ing his food. Lord Coke valued Chaucer highly
because the Canon Yeman's Tale illustrates the
statute fifth *Hen. IV. Chap.* 4, against alchemy.
I saw a man who believed the principal mischiefs
in the English state were derived from the devotion
to musical concerts. A freemason, not long since,
set out to explain to this country that the principal
cause of the success of General Washington was
the aid he derived from the freemasons.

But worse than the harping on one string, Nature
has secured individualism by giving the private
person a high conceit of his weight in the system.
The pest of society is egotists. There are dull and
bright, sacred and profane, coarse and fine egotists.
It is a disease that like influenza falls on all consti-
tutions. In the distemper known to physicians as
chorea, the patient sometimes turns round and continues to spin slowly on one spot. Is egotism a
metaphysical variety of this malady? The man
runs round a ring formed by his own talent, falls
into an admiration of it, and loses relation to the
world. It is a tendency in all minds. One of its
annoying forms is a craving for sympathy. The
sufferers parade their miseries, tear the lint from

their bruises, reveal their indictable crimes, that you may pity them. They like sickness, because physical pain will extort some show of interest from the bystanders, as we have seen children who finding themselves of no account when grown people come in, will cough till they choke, to draw attention.

This distemper is the scourge of talent, — of artists, inventors and philosophers. Eminent spiritualists shall have an incapacity of putting their act or word aloof from them and seeing it bravely for the nothing it is. Beware of the man who says, " I am on the eve of a revelation." It is speedily punished, inasmuch as this habit invites men to humor it, and, by treating the patient tenderly, to shut him up in a narrower selfism and exclude him from the great world of God's cheerful fallible men and women. Let us rather be insulted, whilst we are insultable. Religious literature has eminent examples, and if we run over our private list of poets, critics, philanthropists and philosophers, we shall find them infected with this dropsy and elephantiasis, which we ought to have tapped.

This goitre of egotism is so frequent among notable persons that we must infer some strong necessity in nature which it subserves; such as we see in the sexual attraction. The preservation of the species was a point of such necessity that Nature has secured it at all hazards by immensely overloading the passion, at the risk of perpetual crime and disorder. So egotism has its root in the cardinal necessity by which each individual persists to be what he is.

This individuality is not only not inconsistent with culture, but is the basis of it. Every valuable nature is there in its own right, and the student we speak to must have a motherwit invincible by his culture, — which uses all books, arts, facilities, and elegancies of intercourse, but is never subdued and lost in them. He only is a well-made man who has a good determination. And the end of culture is not to destroy this, God forbid! but to train away all impediment and mixture and leave nothing but pure power. Our student must have a style and determination, and be a master in his own specialty. But having this, he must put it behind him. He must have a catholicity, a power to see with a free and disengaged look every object. Yet is this private interest and self so overcharged that if a man seeks a companion who can look at objects for their own sake and without affection or self-reference, he will find the fewest who will give him that satisfaction; whilst most men are afflicted with a coldness, an incuriosity, as soon as any object does not connect with their self-love. Though they talk of the object before them, they are thinking of themselves, and their vanity is laying little traps for your admiration.

But after a man has discovered that there are limits to the interest which his private history has for mankind, he still converses with his family, or a few companions, — perhaps with half a dozen personalities that are famous in his neighborhood. In Boston the question of life is the names of some eight or ten men. Have you seen Mr. Allston, Doctor Channing, Mr. Adams, Mr. Webster, Mr. Greenough? Have you heard Everett, Garrison, Father Taylor, Theodore Parker? Have you talked with Messieurs Turbinewheel, Summitlevel, and Lacofrupees? Then you may as well die. In New York the question is of some other eight, or ten, or twenty. Have you seen a few lawyers, merchants and brokers, — two or three scholars, two or three capitalists, two or three editors of newspapers? New York is a sucked orange. All conversation is at an end when we have discharged ourselves of a dozen personalities, domestic or imported, which make up our American existence. Nor do we expect anybody to be other than a faint copy of these heroes.

Life is very narrow. Bring any club or company of intelligent men together again after ten years, and if the presence of some penetrating and calming genius could dispose them to frankness, what a confession of insanities would come up! The "causes" to which we have sacrificed, Tariff or Democracy, Whigism or Abolition, Temperance or Socialism would show like roots of bitterness and dragons of wrath; and our talents are as mischievous as if each had been seized upon by some bird of prey which had whisked him away from fortune, from truth, from the dear society of the poets; — some zeal, some bias, and only when he was now gray and nerveless was it relaxing its claws and he awaking to sober perceptions.

Culture is the suggestion, from certain best thoughts, that a man has a range of affinities through which he can modulate the violence of any master-tones that have a droning preponderance in his scale, and succor him against himself. Culture redresses his balance, puts him among his equals and superiors, revives the delicious sense of sympathy and warns him of the dangers of solitude and repulsion.

It is not a compliment but a disparagement to consult a man only on horses, or on steam, or on theatres, or on eating, or on books, and, whenever he appears, considerately to turn the conversation to the bantling he is known to fondle. In the Norse heaven of our forefathers, Thor's house had five hundred and forty floors; and man's house has five hundred and forty floors. His excellence is

facility of adaptation and of transition through
many related points, to wide contrasts and extremes. Culture kills his exaggeration, his conceit
of his village or his city. We must leave our pets
at home when we go into the street, and meet men
on broad grounds of good meaning and good sense.
No performance is worth loss of geniality. 'T is
a cruel price we pay for certain fancy goods called
fine arts and philosophy. In the Norse legend, All-
fadir did not get a drink of Mimir's spring (the
fountain of wisdom) until he left his eye in pledge.
And here is a pedant that cannot unfold his
wrinkles, nor conceal his wrath at interruption by
the best, if their conversation do not fit his imper-
tinency, — here is he to afflict us with his personalities. 'T is incident to scholars that each of
them fancies he is pointedly odious in his community. Draw him out of this limbo of irritability.
Cleanse with healthy blood his parchment skin.
You restore to him his eyes which he left in pledge
at Mimir's spring. If you are the victim of your
doing, who cares what you do? We can spare
your opera, your gazetteer, your chemic analysis,
your history, your syllogisms. Your man of genius
pays dear for his distinction. His head runs up
into a spire, and instead of a healthy man, merry
and wise, he is some mad dominie. Nature is reck-
less of the individual. When she has points to

carry, she carries them. To wade in marshes and sea-margins is the destiny of certain birds, and they are so accurately made for this that they are imprisoned in those places. Each animal out of its *habitat* would starve. To the physician, each man, each woman, is an amplification of one organ. A soldier, a locksmith, a bank-clerk and a dancer could not exchange functions. And thus we are victims of adaptation.

The antidotes against this organic egotism are the range and variety of attractions, as gained by acquaintance with the world, with men of merit, with classes of society, with travel, with eminent persons, and with the high resources of philosophy, art, and religion ; books, travel, society, solitude.

The hardiest skeptic who has seen a horse broken, a pointer trained, or who has visited a menagerie or the exhibition of the Industrious Fleas, will not deny the validity of education. " A boy," says Plato, " is the most vicious of all wild beasts ; " and in the same spirit the old English poet Gascoigne says, " A boy is better unborn than untaught." The city breeds one kind of speech and manners ; the back country a different style ; the sea another ; the army a fourth. We know that an army which can be confided in may be formed by discipline ; that by systematic discipline all men may be made heroes : Marshal Lannes said to a

French officer, " Know, Colonel, that none but a poltroon will boast that he never was afraid." A great part of courage is the courage of having done the thing before. And in all human action those faculties will be strong which are used. Robert Owen said, " Give me a tiger, and I will educate him." 'T is inhuman to want faith in the power of education, since to meliorate is the law of nature ; and men are valued precisely as they exert onward or meliorating force. On the other hand, poltroonery is the acknowledging an inferiority to be incurable.

Incapacity of melioration is the only mortal distemper. There are people who can never understand a trope or any second or expanded sense given to your words, or any humor; but remain literalists, after hearing the music and poetry and rhetoric and wit of seventy or eighty years. They are past the help of surgeon or clergy. But even these can understand pitchforks and the cry of Fire! and I have noticed in some of this class a marked dislike of earthquakes.

Let us make our education brave and preventive. Politics is an after-work, a poor patching. We are always a little late. The evil is done, the law is passed, and we begin the up-hill agitation for repeal of that of which we ought to have prevented the enacting. We shall one day learn to supersede politics by education. What we call our root-and-branch reforms, of slavery, war, gambling, intemperance, is only medicating the symptoms. We must begin higher up, namely in Education.

Our arts and tools give to him who can handle them much the same advantage over the novice as if you extended his life, ten, fifty, or a hundred years. And I think it the part of good sense to provide every fine soul with such culture that it shall not, at thirty or forty years, have to say 'This which I might do is made hopeless through my want of weapons.'

But it is conceded that much of our training fails of effect; that all success is hazardous and rare; that a large part of our cost and pains is thrown away. Nature takes the matter into her own hands, and though we must not omit any jot of our system, we can seldom be sure that it has availed much, or that as much good would not have accrued from a different system.

Books, as containing the finest records of human wit, must always enter into our notion of culture. The best heads that ever existed, Pericles, Plato, Julius Cæsar, Shakspeare, Goethe, Milton, were well-read, universally educated men, and quite too wise to undervalue letters. Their opinion has weight, because they had means of knowing the opposite opinion. We look that a great man should

be a good reader, or in proportion to the spontane-
ous power should be the assimilating power. Good
criticism is very rare and always precious. I am
always happy to meet persons who perceive the
transcendent superiority of Shakspeare over all
other writers. I like people who like Plato. Because this love does not consist with self-conceit.

But books are good only as far as a boy is ready
for them. He sometimes gets ready very slowly.
You send your child to the schoolmaster, but 't is
the schoolboys who educate him. You send him
to the Latin class, but much of his tuition comes,
on his way to school, from the shop-windows. You
like the strict rules and the long terms ; and he
finds his best leading in a by-way of his own, and
refuses any companions but of his choosing. He
hates the grammar and *Gradus*, and loves guns,
fishing-rods, horses, and boats. Well, the boy
is right, and you are not fit to direct his bringing-
up if your theory leaves out his gymnastic training. Archery, cricket, gun and fishing-rod, horse
and boat, are all educators, liberalizers ; and so are
dancing, dress, and the street-talk ; and provided
only the boy has resources, and is of a noble and
ingenuous strain, these will not serve him less than
the books. He learns chess, whist, dancing and
theatricals. The father observes that another boy
has learned algebra and geometry in the same time.

But the first boy has acquired much more than these poor games along with them. He is infatuated for weeks with whist and chess; but presently will find out, as you did, that when he rises from the game too long played, he is vacant and forlorn and despises himself. Thenceforward it takes place with other things, and has its due weight in his experience. These minor skills and accomplishments, for example dancing, are tickets of admission to the dress-circle of mankind, and the being master of them enables the youth to judge intelligently of much on which otherwise he would give a pedantic squint. Landor said, " I have suffered more from my bad dancing than from all the misfortunes and miseries of my life put together." Provided always the boy is teachable (for we are not proposing to make a statue out of punk), football, cricket, archery, swimming, skating, climbing, fencing, riding, are lessons in the art of power, which it is his main business to learn; — riding, specially, of which Lord Herbert of Cherbury said, " A good rider on a good horse is as much above himself and others as the world can make him." Besides, the gun, fishing-rod, boat, and horse, constitute, among all who use them, secret freemasonries. They are as if they belonged to one club.

There is also a negative value in these arts. Their chief use to the youth is not amusement,

but to be known for what they are, and not to remain to him occasions of heart-burn. We are
full of superstitions. Each class fixes its eyes on
the advantages it has not ; the refined, on rude
strength ; the democrat, on birth and breeding.
One of the benefits of a college education is to
show the boy its little avail. I knew a leading
man in a leading city, who, having set his heart
on an education at the university and missed it,
could never quite feel himself the equal of his own
brothers who had gone thither. His easy superiority to multitudes of professional men could never
quite countervail to him this imaginary defect.
Balls, riding, wine-parties and billiards pass to a
poor boy for something fine and romantic, which
they are not ; and a free admission to them on an
equal footing, if it were possible, only once or
twice, would be worth ten times its cost, by undeceiving him.

I am not much an advocate for travelling, and I
observe that men run away to other countries because they are not good in their own, and run back
to their own because they pass for nothing in the
new places. For the most part, only the light char-
acters travel. Who are you that have no task to
keep you at home? I have been quoted as saying
captious things about travel ; but I mean to do justice. I think there is a restlessness in our people

which argues want of character. All educated
Americans, first or last, go to Europe; perhaps because it is their mental home, as the invalid habits
of this country might suggest. An eminent teacher
of girls said, "the idea of a girl's education is,
whatever qualifies her for going to Europe." Can
we never extract this tape-worm of Europe from the
brain of our countrymen? One sees very well what
their fate must be. He that does not fill a place at
home, cannot abroad. He only goes there to hide
his insignificance in a larger crowd. You do not
think you will find anything there which you have
not seen at home? The stuff of all countries is just
the same. Do you suppose there is any country
where they do not scald milk-pans, and swaddle the
infants, and burn the brushwood, and broil the fish?
What is true anywhere is true everywhere. And
let him go where he will, he can only find so much
beauty or worth as he carries.

Of course, for some men, travel may be useful.
Naturalists, discoverers, and sailors are born. Some
men are made for couriers, exchangers, envoys, mis-
sionaries, bearers of despatches, as others are for
farmers and working-men. And if the man is of a
light and social turn, and Nature has aimed to make
a legged and winged creature, framed for locomotion, we must follow her hint and furnish him with
that breeding which gives currency, as sedulously

as with that which gives worth. But let us not be pedantic, but allow to travel its full effect. The boy grown up on a farm, which he has never left, is said in the country to have had *no chance*, and boys and men of that condition look upon work on a railroad, or drudgery in a city, as opportunity. Poor country boys of Vermont and Connecticut formerly owed what knowledge they had to their peddling trips to the Southern States. California and the Pacific Coast is now the university of this class, as Virginia was in old times. ' To have *some chance*' is their word. And the phrase ' to know the world,' or to travel, is synonymous with all men's ideas of advantage and superiority. No doubt, to a man of sense, travel offers advantages. As many languages as he has, as many friends, as many arts and trades, so many times is he a man. A foreign country is a point of comparison where-from to judge his own. One use of travel is to recommend the books and works of home, — we go to Europe to be Americanized; and another, to find men. For as Nature has put fruits apart in latitudes, a new fruit in every degree, so knowledge and fine moral quality she lodges in distant men. And thus, of the six or seven teachers whom each man wants among his contemporaries, it often happens that one or two of them live on the other side of the world.

Moreover, there is in every constitution a certain solstice when the stars stand still in our inward firmament, and when there is required some foreign force, some diversion or alterative to prevent stagnation. And, as a medical remedy, travel seems one of the best. Just as a man witnessing the admirable effect of ether to lull pain, and meditating on the contingencies of wounds, cancers, lockjaws, rejoices in Dr. Jackson's benign discovery, so a man who looks at Paris, at Naples, or at London, says, ' If I should be driven from my own home, here at least my thoughts can be consoled by the most prodigal amusement and occupation which the human race in ages could contrive and accumulate.'

Akin to the benefit of foreign travel, the æsthetic value of railroads is to unite the advantages of town and country life, neither of which we can spare. A man should live in or near a large town, because, let his own genius be what it may, it will repel quite as much of agreeable and valuable talent as it draws, and, in a city, the total attraction of all the citizens is sure to conquer, first or last, every repulsion, and drag the most improbable hermit within its walls some day in the year. In town he can find the swimming - school, the gymnasium, the dancing-master, the shooting-gallery, opera, theatre, and panorama; the chemist's shop, the museum of natural history; the gallery of fine arts; the national orators, in their turn; foreign travellers, the libraries and his club. In the country he can find solitude and reading, manly labor, cheap living, and his old shoes; moors for game, hills for geology and groves for devotion. Aubrey writes, "I have heard Thomas Hobbes say, that, in the Earl of Devon's house, in Derbyshire, there was a good library and books enough for him, and his lordship stored the library with what books he thought fit to be bought. But the want of good conversation was a very great inconvenience, and, though he conceived he could order his thinking as well as another, yet he found a great defect. In the country, in long time, for want of good conversation, one's understanding and invention contract a moss on them, like an old paling in an orchard."

Cities give us collision. It is said, London and New York take the nonsense out of a man. A great part of our education is sympathetic and social. Boys and girls who have been brought up with well-informed and superior people show in their manners an inestimable grace. Fuller says that " William, Earl of Nassau, won a subject from the King of Spain, every time he put off his hat." You cannot have one well-bred man without a whole society of such. They keep each other up to any high point. Especially women; it requires a great many cultivated women, — saloons of bright, elegant, reading women, accustomed to ease and refinement, to spectacles, pictures, sculpture, poetry, and to elegant society, — in order that you should have one Madame de Stael. The head of a commercial house or a leading lawyer or politician is brought into daily contact with troops of men from all parts of the country, and those too the driving-wheels, the business men of each section, and one can hardly suggest for an apprehensive man a more searching culture. Besides, we must remember the high social possibilities of a million of men. The best bribe which London offers to-day to the imagination is that in such a vast variety of people and conditions one can believe there is room for persons of romantic character to exist, and that the poet, the mystic and the hero may hope to confront their counterparts.

I wish cities could teach their best lesson, — of quiet manners. It is the foible especially of American youth, — pretension. The mark of the man of the world is absence of pretension. He does not make a speech, he takes a low business-tone, avoids all brag, is nobody, dresses plainly, promises not at all, performs much, speaks in monosyllables, hugs his fact. He calls his employment by its lowest name, and so takes from evil tongues their sharpest weapon. His conversation clings to the

weather and the news, yet he allows himself to be
surprised into thought and the unlocking of his
learning and philosophy.   How the imagination is
piqued by anecdotes of some great man passing in-
cognito, as a king in gray clothes; of Napoleon
affecting a plain suit at his glittering levee; of
Burns or Scott or Beethoven or Wellington or
Goethe, or any container of transcendent power,
passing for nobody; of Epaminondas, " who never
says anything, but will listen eternally;" of Goethe,
who preferred trifling subjects and common expressions in intercourse with strangers, worse rather
than better clothes, and to appear a little more capricious than he was.   There are advantages in the
old hat and box-coat.   I have heard that throughout this country a certain respect is paid to good
broadcloth; but dress makes a little restraint; men
will not commit themselves.   But the box-coat is
like wine, it unlocks the tongue, and men say what
they think.   An old poet says, —

> " Go far and go sparing,
> For you'll find it certain,
> The poorer and the baser you appear,
> The more you'll look through still." [1]

Not much otherwise Milnes writes in the " Lay of
the Humble," —

[1] Beaumont and Fletcher :   *The Tamer Tamed.*

> " To me men are for what they are,
>   They wear no masks with me."

It is odd that our people should have — not water
on the brain, but a little gas there.   A shrewd foreigner said of the Americans that "whatever they
say has a little the air of a speech."   Yet one of
the traits down in the books as distinguishing the
Anglo-Saxon is a trick of self-disparagement.   To
be sure, in old, dense countries, among a million of
good coats a fine coat comes to be no distinction,
and you find humorists.   In an English party a
man with no marked manners or features, with a
face like red dough, unexpectedly discloses wit,
learning, a wide range of topics and personal fa-
miliarity with good men in all parts of the world,
until you think you have fallen upon some illustrious personage.   Can it be that the American
forest has refreshed some weeds of old Pictish bar-
barism just ready to die out, — the love of the
scarlet feather, of beads and tinsel ?   The Italians
are fond of red clothes, peacock plumes and em-
broidery ; and I remember one rainy morning in
the city of Palermo the street was in a blaze with
scarlet umbrellas.   The English have a plain taste.
The equipages of the grandees are plain.   A gor-
geous livery indicates new and awkward city wealth.
Mr. Pitt, like Mr. Pym, thought the title of *Mister*
good against any king in Europe.   They have

piqued themselves on governing the whole world in the poor, plain, dark Committee-room which the House of Commons sat in, before the fire.

Whilst we want cities as the centres where the best things are found, cities degrade us by magnifying trifles. The countryman finds the town a chop-house, a barber's shop. He has lost the lines of grandeur of the horizon, hills, and plains, and with them sobriety and elevation. He has come among a supple, glib-tongued tribe, who live for show, servile to public opinion. Life is dragged down to a fracas of pitiful cares and disasters. You say the gods ought to respect a life whose objects are their own; but in cities they have betrayed you to a cloud of insignificant annoyances : —

> " Mirmidons, race féconde,
>   Mirmidons,
>   Enfin nous commandons :
>   Jupiter livre le monde
>   Aux mirmidons, aux mirmidons." [1]

> 'T is heavy odds
> Against the gods,
> When they will match with myrmidons.
> We spawning, spawning myrmidons,
> Our turn to-day ! we take command,
> Jove gives the globe into the hand
> Of myrmidons, of myrmidons.

[1] Béranger.

What is odious but noise, and people who scream
and bewail? people whose vane points always east,
who live to dine, who send for the doctor, who
coddle themselves, who toast their feet on the reg-
ister, who intrigue to secure a padded chair and a
corner out of the draught. Suffer them once to
begin the enumeration of their infirmities and the
sun will go down on the unfinished tale. Let
these triflers put us out of conceit with petty com-
forts. To a man at work, the frost is but a color;
the rain, the wind, he forgot them when he came in.
Let us learn to live coarsely, dress plainly, and lie
hard. The least habit of dominion over the palate
has certain good effects not easily estimated. Neither will we be driven into a quiddling abstemious-
ness. 'Tis a superstition to insist on a special diet.
All is made at last of the same chemical atoms.

A man in pursuit of greatness feels no little
wants. How can you mind diet, bed, dress, or
salutes or compliments, or the figure you make in
company, or wealth, or even the bringing things
to pass, — when you think how paltry are the
machinery and the workers? Wordsworth was
praised to me in Westmoreland for having af-
forded to his country neighbors an example of a
modest household where comfort and culture were
secured without display. And a tender boy who
wears his rusty cap and outgrown coat, that he

may secure the coveted place in college and the right in the library, is educated to some purpose. There is a great deal of self-denial and manliness in poor and middle-class houses in town and country, that has not got into literature and never will, but that keeps the earth sweet; that saves on superfluities, and spends on essentials; that goes rusty and educates the boy; that sells the horse but builds the school; works early and late, takes two looms in the factory, three looms, six looms, but pays off the mortgage on the paternal farm, and then goes back cheerfully to work again.

We can ill spare the commanding social benefits of cities; they must be used, yet cautiously and haughtily, — and will yield their best values to him who best can do without them. Keep the town for occasions, but the habits should be formed to retirement. Solitude, the safeguard of mediocrity, is, to genius, the stern friend, the cold, obscure shelter where moult the wings which will bear it farther than suns and stars. He who should inspire and lead his race must be defended from travelling with the souls of other men, from living, breathing, reading and writing in the daily, timeworn yoke of their opinions. " In the morning, — solitude ; " said Pythagoras ; that Nature may speak to the imagination, as she does never in company, and that her favorite may make ac-

quaintance with those divine strengths which dis-
close themselves to serious and abstracted thought.
'Tis very certain that Plato, Plotinus, Archimedes,
Hermes, Newton, Milton, Wordsworth, did not
live in a crowd, but descended into it from time to
time as benefactors; and the wise instructor will
press this point of securing to the young soul in
the disposition of time and the arrangements of
living, periods and habits of solitude. The high
advantage of university life is often the mere mechanical one, I may call it, of a separate chamber
and fire, — which parents will allow the boy without hesitation at Cambridge, but do not think
needful at home. We say solitude, to mark the
character of the tone of thought; but if it can be
shared between two or more than two, it is happier
and not less noble. " We four," wrote Neander to
his sacred friends, " will enjoy at Halle the inward
blessedness of a *civitas Dei*, whose foundations are
forever friendship. The more I know you, the
more I dissatisfy and must dissatisfy all my wonted
companions. Their very presence stupefies me.
The common understanding withdraws itself from
the one centre of all existence."

Solitude takes off the pressure of present impor-
tunities, that more catholic and humane relations
may appear. The saint and poet seek privacy to
ends the most public and universal, and it is the

secret of culture to interest the man more in his public than in his private quality. Here is a new poem, which elicits a good many comments in the journals and in conversation. From these it is easy at last to gather the verdict which readers passed upon it; and that is, in the main, unfavorable. The poet, as a craftsman, is only interested in the praise accorded to him, and not in the censure, though it be just. And the poor little poet hearkens only to that, and rejects the censure as proving incapacity in the critic. But the poet *cultivated* becomes a stockholder in both companies, — say Mr. Curfew in the Curfew stock, and in the *humanity* stock; — and, in the last, exults as much in the demonstration of the unsoundness of Curfew, as his interest in the former gives him pleasure in the currency of Curfew. For the depreciation of his Curfew stock only shows the immense values of the humanity stock. As soon as he sides with his critic against himself, with joy, he is a cultivated man.

We must have an intellectual quality in all property and in all action, or they are naught. I must have children, I must have events, I must have a social state and history, or my thinking and speaking want body or basis. But to give these accessories any value, I must know them as contingent and rather showy possessions, which pass for more to the people than to me. We see this abstraction in scholars, as a matter of course; but what a charm it adds when observed in practical men. Bonaparte, like Cæsar, was intellectual, and could look at every object for itself, without affection. Though an egotist *à outrance*, he could criticize a play, a building, a character, on universal grounds, and give a just opinion. A man known to us only as a celebrity in politics or in trade gains largely in our esteem if we discover that he has some intellectual taste or skill; as when we learn of Lord Fairfax, the Long Parliament's general, his passion for antiquarian studies; or of the French regicide Carnot, his sublime genius in mathematics; or of a living banker, his success in poetry; or of a partisan journalist, his devotion to ornithology. So, if in travelling in the dreary wildernesses of Arkansas or Texas we should observe on the next seat a man reading Horace, or Martial, or Calderon, we should wish to hug him.

We only vary the phrase, not the doctrine, when we say that culture opens the sense of beauty. A man is a beggar who only lives to the useful, and however he may serve as a pin or rivet in the social machine, cannot be said to have arrived at self-possession. I suffer every day from the want of perception of beauty in people. They do not know the charm with which all moments and objects can be embellished, the charm of manners, of self-command, of benevolence. Repose and cheerfulness are the badge of the gentleman, — repose in energy. The Greek battle-pieces are calm ; the heroes, in whatever violent actions engaged, retain a serene aspect ; as we say of Niagara that it falls without speed. A cheerful intelligent face is the end of culture, and success enough. For it indicates the purpose of Nature and wisdom attained.

When our higher faculties are in activity we are domesticated, and awkwardness and discomfort give place to natural and agreeable movements. It is noticed that the consideration of the great periods and spaces of astronomy induces a dignity of mind and an indifference to death. The influence of fine scenery, the presence of mountains, appeases our irritations and elevates our friendships. Even a high dome, and the expansive interior of a cathedral, have a sensible effect on manners. I have heard that stiff people lose something of their awkwardness under high ceilings and in spacious halls. I think sculpture and painting have an effect to teach us manners and abolish hurry.

But, over all, culture must reinforce from higher influx the empirical skills of eloquence, or of politics, or of trade and the useful arts. There is a certain loftiness of thought and power to marshal and adjust particulars, which can only come from an insight of their whole connection. The orator who has once seen things in their divine order will never quite lose sight of this, and will come to affairs as from a higher ground, and though he will say nothing of philosophy, he will have a certain mastery in dealing with them, and an incapableness of being dazzled or frighted, which will distinguish his handling from that of attorneys and factors. A man who stands on a good footing with the heads of parties at Washington, reads the rumors of the newspapers and the guesses of provincial politicians with a key to the right and wrong in each statement, and sees well enough where all this will end. Archimedes will look through your Connecticut machine at a glance, and judge of its fitness. And much more a wise man who knows not only what Plato, but what Saint John can show him, can easily raise the affair he deals with to a certain majesty. Plato says Pericles owed this elevation to the lessons of Anaxagoras. Burke descended from a higher sphere when he would influence human affairs. Franklin, Adams, Jefferson, Washington, stood on a fine humanity, before which the brawls of modern senates are but pothouse politics.

But there are higher secrets of culture, which are not for the apprentices but for proficients. These are lessons only for the brave. We must know our friends under ugly masks. The calamities are our friends. Ben Jonson specifies in his address to the Muse : —

> "Get him the time's long grudge, the court's ill-will,
> And, reconciled, keep him suspected still,
> Make him lose all his friends, and, what is worse,
> Almost all ways to any better course ;
> With me thou leav'st a better Muse than thee,
> And which thou brought'st me, blessed Poverty."

We wish to learn philosophy by rote, and play at heroism. But the wiser God says, Take the shame, the poverty and the penal solitude that belong to truth-speaking. Try the rough water as well as the smooth. Rough water can teach lessons worth knowing. When the state is unquiet, personal qualities are more than ever decisive. Fear not a revolution which will constrain you to live five years in one. Don't be so tender at making an enemy now and then. Be willing to go to Coventry sometimes, and let the populace bestow on you their coldest contempts. The finished man of the world must eat of every apple once. He must hold his hatreds also at arm's length, and not remember spite. He has neither friends nor enemies, but values men only as channels of power.

He who aims high must dread an easy home and popular manners. Heaven sometimes hedges a rare character about with ungainliness and odium, as the burr that protects the fruit. If there is any great and good thing in store for you, it will not come at the first or the second call, nor in the shape of fashion, ease, and city drawing-rooms. Popularity is for dolls. " Steep and craggy," said Porphyry, "is the path of the gods." Open your Marcus Antoninus. In the opinion of the ancients he was the great man who scorned to shine, and who contested the frowns of fortune. They preferred the noble vessel too late for the tide, contending with winds and waves, dismantled and unrigged, to her companion borne into harbor with colors flying and guns firing. There is none of the social goods that may not be purchased too dear, and mere amiableness must not take rank with high aims and self-subsistency.

Bettine replies to Goethe's mother, who chides her disregard of dress, — "If I cannot do as I have a mind in our poor Frankfort, I shall not carry things far." And the youth must rate at its true mark the inconceivable levity of local opinion. The longer we live the more we must endure the elementary existence of men and women ; and every brave heart must treat society as a child, and never allow it to dictate.

" All that class of the severe and restrictive virtues," said Burke, " are almost too costly for humanity." Who wishes to be severe ? Who wishes

to resist the eminent and polite, in behalf of the
poor, and low, and impolite ? And who that dares
do it can keep his temper sweet, his frolic spirits ?
The high virtues are not debonair, but have their
redress in being illustrious at last. What forests
of laurel we bring, and the tears of mankind, to
those who stood firm against the opinion of their
contemporaries ! The measure of a master is his
success in bringing all men round to his opinion
twenty years later.

Let me say here, that culture cannot begin too
early. In talking with scholars I observe that they
lost on ruder companions those years of boyhood
which alone could give imaginative literature a religious and infinite quality in their esteem. I find
too that the chance for appreciation is much increased by being the son of an appreciator, and that
these boys who now grow up are caught not only
years too late, but two or three births too late, to
make the best scholars of. And I think it a pre-
sentable motive to a scholar, that, as in an old community a well-born proprietor is usually found,
after the first heats of youth, to be a careful husband, and to feel a habitual desire that the estate
shall suffer no harm by his administration, but
shall be delivered down to the next heir in as good
condition as he received it ; — so a considerate
man will reckon himself a subject of that secular

melioration by which mankind is mollified, cured, and refined; and will shun every expenditure of his forces on pleasure or gain which will jeopardize this social and secular accumulation.

The fossil strata show us that Nature began with rudimental forms and rose to the more complex as fast as the earth was fit for their dwelling-place; and that the lower perish as the higher appear. Very few of our race can be said to be yet finished men. We still carry sticking to us some remains of the preceding inferior quadruped organization. We call these millions men; but they are not yet men. Half-engaged in the soil, pawing to get free, man needs all the music that can be brought to disengage him. If Love, red Love, with tears and joy; if Want with his scourge; if War with his cannonade; if Christianity with its charity: if Trade with its money; if Art with its portfolios; if Science with her telegraphs through the deeps of space and time can set his dull nerves throbbing, and by loud taps on the tough chrysalis can break its walls and let the new creature emerge erect and free, — make way and sing pæan! The age of the quadruped is to go out, the age of the brain and of the heart is to come in. The time will come when the evil forms we have known can no more be organized. Man's culture can spare nothing, wants all the material. He is to convert all impediments into instruments, all enemies into power. The formidable mischief will only make the more useful slave. And if one shall read the future of the race hinted in the organic effort of Nature to mount and meliorate, and the corresponding impulse to the Better in the human being, we shall dare affirm that there is nothing he will not overcome and convert, until at last culture shall absorb the chaos and gehenna. He will convert the Furies into Muses, and the hells into benefit.

V.

BEHAVIOR.

Grace, Beauty, and Caprice
Build this golden portal,
Graceful women, chosen men
Dazzle every mortal:
Their sweet and lofty countenance
His enchanting food;
He need not go to them, their forms
Beset his solitude.
He looketh seldom in their face,
His eyes explore the ground,
The green grass is a looking-glass
Whereon their traits are found.
Little he says to them,
So dances his heart in his breast,
Their tranquil mien bereaveth him
Of wit, of words, of rest.
Too weak to win, too fond to shun
The tyrants of his doom,
The much deceived Endymion
Slips behind a tomb.

BEHAVIOR.

THE soul which animates Nature is not less significantly published in the figure, movement and gesture of animated bodies, than in its last vehicle of articulate speech. This silent and subtile language is Manners; not *what*, but *how*. Life expresses. A statue has no tongue, and needs none. Good tableaux do not need declamation. Nature tells every secret once. Yes, but in man she tells it all the time, by form, attitude, gesture, mien, face and parts of the face, and by the whole action of the machine. The visible carriage or action of the individual, as resulting from his organization and his will combined, we call manners. What are they but thought entering the hands and feet, controlling the movements of the body, the speech and behavior?

There is always a best way of doing everything, if it be to boil an egg. Manners are the happy way of doing things; each, once a stroke of genius or of love, now repeated and hardened into usage. They form at last a rich varnish with which the routine of life is washed and its details adorned. If they are superficial, so are the dew drops which give such a depth to the morning meadows. Manners are very communicable; men catch them from each other. Consuelo, in the romance, boasts of the lessons she had given the nobles in manners, on the stage; and in real life, Talma taught Napoleon the arts of behavior. Genius invents fine manners, which the baron and the baroness copy very fast, and, by the advantage of a palace, better the instruction. They stereotype the lesson they have learned, into a mode.

The power of manners is incessant, — an element as unconcealable as fire. The nobility cannot in any country be disguised, and no more in a republic or a democracy than in a kingdom. No man can resist their influence. There are certain manners which are learned in good society, of that force that if a person have them, he or she must be considered, and is everywhere welcome, though without beauty, or wealth, or genius. Give a boy address and accomplishments and you give him the mastery of palaces and fortunes where he goes. He has not the trouble of earning or owning them, they solicit him to enter and possess. We send girls of a timid, retreating disposition to the boarding-school, to the riding-school, to the ball-room, or wheresoever they can come into acquaintance and nearness of leading persons of their own sex; where they may learn address, and see it near at hand.

The power of a woman of fashion to lead and also to daunt and repel, derives from their belief that she knows resources and behaviors not known to them; but when these have mastered her secret they learn to confront her, and recover their self-possession.

Every day bears witness to their gentle rule. People who would obtrude, now do not obtrude. The mediocre circle learns to demand that which belongs to a high state of nature or of culture. Your manners are always under examination, and by committees little suspected, a police in citizens' clothes, who are awarding or denying you very high prizes when you least think of it.

We talk much of utilities, but 'tis our manners that associate us. In hours of business we go to him who knows, or has, or does this or that which we want, and we do not let our taste or feeling stand in the way. But this activity over, we return to the indolent state, and wish for those we can be at ease with; those who will go where we go, whose manners do not offend us, whose social tone chimes with ours. When we reflect on their persuasive and cheering force; how they recommend, prepare, and draw people together; how, in all clubs, manners make the members; how manners make the fortune of the ambitious youth; that, for the most part, his manners marry him, and, for

the most part, he marries manners; when we think
what keys they are, and to what secrets; what high
lessons and inspiring tokens of character they con-
vey, and what divination is required in us for the
reading of this fine telegraph, — we see what range
the subject has, and what relations to convenience,
power and beauty.

Their first service is very low, — when they are
the minor morals; but 't is the beginning of civility,
— to make us, I mean, endurable to each other.
We prize them for their rough-plastic, abstergent
force; to get people out of the quadruped state; to
get them washed, clothed, and set up on end; to
slough their animal husks and habits; compel them
to be clean; overawe their spite and meanness;
teach them to stifle the base and choose the generous expression, and make them know how much
happier the generous behaviors are.

Bad behavior the laws cannot reach. Society is
infested with rude, cynical, restless and frivolous
persons, who prey upon the rest, and whom a public opinion concentrated into good manners — forms
accepted by the sense of all — can reach : the contradictors and railers at public and private tables,
who are like terriers, who conceive it the duty of a
dog of honor to growl at any passer-by and do the
honors of the house by barking him out of sight. I
have seen men who neigh like a horse when you

contradict them or say something which they do not understand : — then the overbold, who make their own invitation to your hearth ; the persevering talker, who gives you his society in large saturating doses ; the pitiers of themselves, a perilous class ; the frivolous Asmodeus, who relies on you to find him in ropes of sand to twist ; the monotones ; in short, every stripe of absurdity ; — these are social inflictions which the magistrate cannot cure or defend you from, and which must be intrusted to the restraining force of custom and proverbs and familiar rules of behavior impressed on young people in their school-days.

In the hotels on the banks of the Mississippi they print, or used to print, among the rules of the house, that " No gentleman can be permitted to come to the public table without his coat ; " and in the same country, in the pews of the churches little placards plead with the worshipper against the fury of expectoration. Charles Dickens self-sacrificingly undertook the reformation of our American manners in unspeakable particulars. I think the lesson was not quite lost ; that it held bad manners up, so that the churls could see the deformity. Unhappily the book had its own deformities. It ought not to need to print in a reading-room a caution to strangers not to speak loud ; nor to persons who look over fine engravings that they should be handled like cobwebs and butterflies' wings; nor to persons who look at marble statues that they shall not smite them with canes. But even in the perfect civilization of this city such cautions are not quite needless in the Athenæum and City Library.

Manners are factitious, and grow out of circumstance as well as out of character. If you look at the pictures of patricians and of peasants of different periods and countries, you will see how well they match the same classes in our towns. The modern aristocrat not only is well drawn in Titian's Venetian doges and in Roman coins and statues, but also in the pictures which Commodore Perry brought home of dignitaries in Japan. Broad lands and great interests not only arrive to such heads as can manage them, but form manners of power. A keen eye too will see nice gradations of rank, or see in the manners the degree of homage the party is wont to receive. A prince who is accustomed every day to be courted and deferred to by the highest grandees, acquires a corresponding expectation and a becoming mode of receiving and replying to this homage.

There are always exceptional people and modes. English grandees affect to be farmers. Claverhouse is a fop, and under the finish of dress and levity of behavior hides the terror of his war. But

Nature and Destiny are honest, and never fail to leave their mark, to hang out a sign for each and for every quality. It is much to conquer one's face, and perhaps the ambitious youth thinks he has got the whole secret when he has learned that disengaged manners are commanding. Don't be deceived by a facile exterior. Tender men sometimes have strong wills. We had in Massachusetts an old statesman who had sat all his life in courts and in chairs of state without overcoming an extreme irritability of face, voice, and bearing; when he spoke, his voice would not serve him; it cracked, it broke, it wheezed, it piped ;— little cared he; he knew that it had got to pipe, or wheeze, or screech his argument and his indignation. When he sat down, after speaking, he seemed in a sort of fit, and held on to his chair with both hands : but underneath all this irritability was a puissant will, firm and advancing, and a memory in which lay in order and method like geologic strata every fact of his history, and under the control of his will.

Manners are partly factitious, but mainly there must be capacity for culture in the blood. Else all culture is vain. The obstinate prejudice in favor of blood, which lies at the base of the feudal and monarchical fabrics of the Old World, has some reason in common experience. Every man, — mathematician, artist, soldier, or merchant, — looks with

confidence for some traits and talents in his own
child which he would not dare to presume in the
child of a stranger. The Orientalists are very orthodox on this point. " Take a thorn-bush," said
the emir Abdel-Kader, "and sprinkle it for a whole
year with water;—it will yield nothing but thorns.
Take a date-tree, leave it without culture, and it
will always produce dates. Nobility is the date-
tree and the Arab populace is a bush of thorns."

A main fact in the history of manners is the
wonderful expressiveness of the human body. If
it were made of glass, or of air, and the thoughts
were written on steel tablets within, it could not
publish more truly its meaning than now. Wise
men read very sharply all your private history in
your look and gait and behavior. The whole economy of nature is bent on expression. The tell-tale
body is all tongues. Men are like Geneva watches
with crystal faces which expose the whole movement. They carry the liquor of life flowing up and
down in these beautiful bottles and announcing to
the curious how it is with them. The face and
eyes reveal what the spirit is doing, how old it is,
what aims it has. The eyes indicate the antiquity
of the soul, or through how many forms it has
already ascended. It almost violates the proprieties if we say above the breath here what the con-
fessing eyes do not hesitate to utter to every street
passenger.

Man cannot fix his eye on the sun, and so far seems imperfect. In Siberia a late traveller found men who could see the satellites of Jupiter with their unarmed eye. In some respects the animals excel us. The birds have a longer sight, beside the advantage by their wings of a higher observatory. A cow can bid her calf, by secret signal, probably of the eye, to run away or to lie down and hide itself. The jockeys say of certain horses that "they look over the whole ground." The out-door life and hunting and labor give equal vigor to the human eye. A farmer looks out at you as strong as the horse; his eye-beam is like the stroke of a staff. An eye can threaten like a loaded and levelled gun, or can insult like hissing or kicking; or in its altered mood by beams of kindness it can make the heart dance with joy.

The eye obeys exactly the action of the mind. When a thought strikes us, the eyes fix and remain gazing at a distance; in enumerating the names of persons or of countries, as France, Germany, Spain, Turkey, the eyes wink at each new name. There is no nicety of learning sought by the mind which the eyes do not vie in acquiring. "An artist," said Michael Angelo, "must have his measuring tools not in the hand, but in the eye;" and there is no end to the catalogue of its performances, whether in indolent vision (that of health and beauty), or in strained vision (that of art and labor).

Eyes are bold as lions, — roving, running, leaping, here and there, far and near. They speak all languages. They wait for no introduction; they are no Englishmen; ask no leave of age, or rank; they respect neither poverty nor riches, neither learning nor power nor virtue nor sex; but intrude, and come again, and go through and through you in a moment of time. What inundation of life and thought is discharged from one soul into another, through them! The glance is natural magic. The mysterious communication established across a house between two entire strangers, moves all the springs of wonder. The communication by the glance is in the greatest part not subject to the control of the will. It is the bodily symbol of identity of nature. We look into the eyes to know if this other form is another self, and the eyes will not lie, but make a faithful confession what inhabitant is there. The revelations are sometimes terrific. The confession of a low, usurping devil is there made, and the observer shall seem to feel the stirring of owls and bats and horned hoofs, where he looked for innocence and simplicity. 'T is remarkable too that the spirit that appears at the windows of the house does at once invest himself in a new form of his own to the mind of the beholder.

The eyes of men converse as much as their tongues, with the advantage that the ocular dialect needs no dictionary, but is understood all the world over. When the eyes say one thing and the tongue another, a practised man relies on the language of the first. If the man is off his centre, the eyes show it. You can read in the eyes of your companion whether your argument hits him, though his tongue will not confess it. There is a look by which a man shows he is going to say a good thing, and a look when he has said it. Vain and forgotten are all the fine offers and offices of hospitality, if there is no holiday in the eye. How many furtive inclinations avowed by the eye, though dissembled by the lips! One comes away from a company in which, it may easily happen, he has said nothing and no important remark has been addressed to him, and yet, if in sympathy with the society, he shall not have a sense of this fact, such a stream of life has been flowing into him and out from him through the eyes. There are eyes, to be sure, that give no more admission into the man than blueberries. Others are liquid and deep, — wells that a man might fall into; — others are aggressive and devouring, seem to call out the police, take all too much notice, and require crowded Broadways and the security of millions to protect individuals against them. The military eye

I meet, now darkly sparkling under clerical, now under rustic brows. 'T is the city of Lacedæmon; 't is a stack of bayonets. There are asking eyes, asserting eyes, prowling eyes; and eyes full of fate, — some of good and some of sinister omen. The alleged power to charm down insanity, or ferocity in beasts, is a power behind the eye. It must be a victory achieved in the will, before it can be signified in the eye. It is very certain that each man carries in his eye the exact indication of his rank in the immense scale of men, and we are always learning to read it. A complete man should need no auxiliaries to his personal presence. Whoever looked on him would consent to his will, being certified that his aims were generous and universal. The reason why men do not obey us is because they see the mud at the bottom of our eye.

If the organ of sight is such a vehicle of power, the other features have their own. A man finds room in the few square inches of the face for the traits of all his ancestors; for the expression of all his history and his wants. The sculptor and Winckelmann and Lavater will tell you how significant a feature is the nose ; how its forms express strength or weakness of will, and good or bad temper. The nose of Julius Cæsar, of Dante, and of Pitt, suggest " the terrors of the beak." What refinement and what limitations the teeth betray !

" Beware you don't laugh," said the wise mother,
" for then you show all your faults."

Balzac left in manuscript a chapter which he
called " *Théorie de la démarche*," in which he
says, " The look, the voice, the respiration, and the
attitude or walk, are identical. But, as it has not
been given to man the power to stand guard at
once over these four different simultaneous expressions of his thought, watch that one which speaks
out the truth, and you will know the whole man."

Palaces interest us mainly in the exhibition of
manners, which, in the idle and expensive society
dwelling in them, are raised to a high art. The
maxim of courts is that manner is power. A calm
and resolute bearing, a polished speech, an embel-
lishment of trifles, and the art of hiding all uncomfortable feeling, are essential to the courtier ; and
Saint Simon and Cardinal de Retz and Rœderer
and an encyclopædia of *Mémoires* will instruct you,
if you wish, in those potent secrets. Thus it is a
point of pride with kings to remember faces and
names. It is reported of one prince that his head
had the air of leaning downwards, in order not to
humble the crowd. There are people who come in
ever like a child with a piece of good news. It
was said of the late Lord Holland that he always
came down to breakfast with the air of a man who
had just met with some signal good-fortune. In

" *Nôtre Dame*," the grandee took his place on the dais with the look of one who is thinking of something else. But we must not peep and eavesdrop at palace-doors.

Fine manners need the support of fine manners in others. A scholar may be a well-bred man, or he may not. The enthusiast is introduced to polished scholars in society and is chilled and silenced by finding himself not in their element. They all have somewhat which he has not, and, it seems, ought to have. But if he finds the scholar apart from his companions, it is then the enthusiast's turn, and the scholar has no defence, but must deal on his terms. Now they must fight the battle out on their private strength. What is the talent of that character so common — the successful man of the world — in all marts, senates, and drawing-rooms? Manners: manners of power; sense to see his advantage, and manners up to it. See him approach his man. He knows that troops behave as they are handled at first; that is his cheap secret; just what happens to every two persons who meet on any affair, — one instantly perceives that he has the key of the situation, that his will comprehends the other's will, as the cat does the mouse; and he has only to use courtesy and furnish good-natured reasons to his victim to cover up the chain, lest he be shamed into resistance.

The theatre in which this science of manners
has a formal importance is not with us a court, but
dress-circles, wherein, after the close of the day's
business, men and women meet at leisure, for mutual entertainment, in ornamented drawing-rooms.
Of course it has every variety of attraction and
merit; but to earnest persons, to youths or maidens
who have great objects at heart, we cannot extol it
highly. A well-dressed talkative company where
each is bent to amuse the other, — yet the high-born
Turk who came hither fancied that every woman
seemed to be suffering for a chair; that all the
talkers were brained and exhausted by the deoxy-
genated air; it spoiled the best persons; it put
all on stilts. Yet here are the secret biographies
written and read. The aspect of that man is repul-
sive; I do not wish to deal with him. The other
is irritable, shy, and on his guard. The youth
looks humble and manly; I choose him. Look on
this woman. There is not beauty, nor brilliant
sayings, nor distinguished power to serve you; but
all see her gladly; her whole air and impression
are healthful. Here come the sentimentalists, and
the invalids. Here is Elise, who caught cold in
coming into the world and has always increased it
since. Here are creep-mouse manners, and thiev-
ish manners. "Look at Northcote," said Fuseli;
" he looks like a rat that has seen a cat." In the

shallow company, easily excited, easily tired, here is the columnar Bernard; the Alleghanies do not express more repose than his behavior. Here are the sweet following eyes of Cecile; it seemed always that she demanded the heart. Nothing can be more excellent in kind than the Corinthian grace of Gertrude's manners, and yet Blanche, who has no manners, has better manners than she; for the movements of Blanche are the sallies of a spirit which is sufficient for the moment, and she can afford to express every thought by instant action.

Manners have been somewhat cynically defined to be a contrivance of wise men to keep fools at a distance. Fashion is shrewd to detect those who do not belong to her train, and seldom wastes her attentions. Society is very swift in its instincts, and, if you do not belong to it, resists and sneers at you, or quietly drops you. The first weapon enrages the party attacked; the second is still more effective, but is not to be resisted, as the date of the transaction is not easily found. People grow up and grow old under this infliction, and never suspect the truth, ascribing the solitude which acts on them very injuriously to any cause but the right one.

The basis of good manners is self-reliance. Necessity is the law of all who are not self-possessed. Those who are not self-possessed obtrude and pain us. Some men appear to feel that they belong to a Pariah caste. They fear to offend, they bend and apologize, and walk through life with a timid step. As we sometimes dream that we are in a well-dressed company without any coat, so Godfrey acts ever as if he suffered from some mortifying circumstance. The hero should find himself at home, wherever he is; should impart comfort by his own security and good-nature to all beholders. The hero is suffered to be himself. A person of strong mind comes to perceive that for him an immunity is secured so long as he renders to society that service which is native and proper to him, — an immunity from all the observances, yea, and duties, which society so tyrannically imposes on the rank and file of its members. " Euripides," says Aspasia, " has not the fine manners of Sophocles; but," she adds good-humoredly, " the movers and masters of our souls have surely a right to throw out their limbs as carelessly as they please, on the world that belongs to them, and before the creatures they have animated." [1]

Manners require time, as nothing is more vulgar than haste. Friendship should be surrounded with ceremonies and respects, and not crushed into corners. Friendship requires more time than poor busy men can usually command. Here comes to

[1] Landor : *Pericles and Aspasia.*

me Roland, with a delicacy of sentiment leading
and inwrapping him like a divine cloud or holy
ghost. 'T is a great destitution to both that this
should not be entertained with large leisures, but
contrariwise should be balked by importunate affairs.

But through this lustrous varnish the reality is
ever shining. 'T is hard to keep the *what* from
breaking through this pretty painting of the *how*.
The core will come to the surface. Strong will
and keen perception overpower old manners and
create new; and the thought of the present moment has a greater value than all the past. In
persons of character we do not remark manners,
because of their instantaneousness. We are surprised by the thing done, out of all power to watch
the way of it. Yet nothing is more charming than
to recognize the great style which runs through
the actions of such. People masquerade before us
in their fortunes, titles, offices, and connections, as
academic or civil presidents, or senators, or professors, or great lawyers, and impose on the frivolous,
and a good deal on each other, by these fames. At
least it is a point of prudent good manners to treat
these reputations tenderly, as if they were merited.
But the sad realist knows these fellows at a glance,
and they know him; as when in Paris the chief
of the police enters a ball-room, so many diamonded

pretenders shrink and make themselves as incon-
spicuous as they can, or give him a supplicating
look as they pass. " I had received," said a sibyl,
" I had received at birth the fatal gift of penetration ; " and these Cassandras are always born.

Manners impress as they indicate real power. A
man who is sure of his point, carries a broad and
contented expression, which everybody reads. And
you cannot rightly train one to an air and manner,
except by making him the kind of man of whom
that manner is the natural expression. Nature forever puts a premium on reality. What is done for
effect is seen to be done for effect; what is done
for love is felt to be done for love. A man inspires
affection and honor because he was not lying in
wait for these. The things of a man for which we
visit him were done in the dark and the cold. A
little integrity is better than any career. So deep
are the sources of this surface-action that even the
size of your companion seems to vary with his freedom of thought. Not only is he larger, when at
ease and his thoughts generous, but every thing
around him becomes variable with expression. No
carpenter's rule, no rod and chain will measure the
dimensions of any house or house-lot ; go into the
house ; if the proprietor is constrained and defer-
ring 'tis of no importance how large his house, how
beautiful his grounds, — you quickly come to the

end of all : but if the man is self-possessed, happy and at home, his house is deep-founded, indefinitely large and interesting, the roof and dome buoyant as the sky. Under the humblest roof, the commonest person in plain clothes sits there massive, cheerful, yet formidable, like the Egyptian colossi.

Neither Aristotle, nor Leibnitz, nor Junius, nor Champollion has set down the grammar-rules of this dialect, older than Sanscrit; but they who cannot yet read English, can read this. Men take each other's measure, when they meet for the first time, — and every time they meet. How do they get this rapid knowledge, even before they speak, of each other's power and dispositions ? One would say that the persuasion of their speech is not in what they say, — or that men do not convince by their argument, but by their personality, by who they are, and what they said and did heretofore. A man already strong is listened to, and every thing he says is applauded. Another opposes him with sound argument, but the argument is scouted until by and by it gets into the mind of some weighty person; then it begins to tell on the community.

Self-reliance is the basis of behavior, as it is the guaranty that the powers are not squandered in too much demonstration. In this country, where school education is universal, we have a superficial culture, and a profusion of reading and writing and expression. We parade our nobilities in poems and orations, instead of working them up into happiness. There is a whisper out of the ages to him who can understand it, — " Whatever is known to thyself alone, has always very great value." There is some reason to believe that when a man does not write his poetry it escapes by other vents through him, instead of the one vent of writing; clings to his form and manners, whilst poets have often nothing poetical about them except their verses. Jacobi said that " when a man has fully expressed his thought, he has somewhat less possession of it." One would say, the rule is, — What a man is irresistibly urged to say, helps him and us. In explaining his thought to others, he explains it to himself, but when he opens it for show, it corrupts him.

Society is the stage on which manners are shown ; novels are their literature. Novels are the journal or record of manners, and the new importance of these books derives from the fact that the novelist begins to penetrate the surface and treat this part of life more worthily. The novels used to be all alike, and had a quite vulgar tone. The novels used to lead us on to a foolish interest in the fortunes of the boy and girl they described. The boy was to be raised from a humble to a high position. He was in want of a wife and a castle, and the object of the story was to supply him with one or both. We watched sympathetically, step by step, his climbing, until at last the point is gained, the wedding day is fixed, and we follow the gala procession home to the bannered portal, when the doors are slammed in our face and the poor reader is left outside in the cold, not enriched by so much as an idea or a virtuous impulse.

But the victories of character are instant, and victories for all. Its greatness enlarges all. We are fortified by every heroic anecdote. The novels are as useful as Bibles if they teach you the secret that the best of life is conversation, and the greatest success is confidence, or perfect understanding between sincere people. 'T is a French definition of friendship, *rien que s'entendre*, good understanding. The highest compact we can make with our fellow, is, — 'Let there be truth between us two forevermore.' That is the charm in all good novels, as it is the charm in all good histories, that the heroes mutually understand, from the first, and deal loyally and with a profound trust in each other. It is sublime to feel and say of another, I need never meet or speak or write to him; we need not reinforce ourselves, or send tokens of remembrance; I rely on him as on myself; if he did thus or thus, I know it was right.

In all the superior people I have met I notice directness, truth spoken more truly, as if everything of obstruction, of malformation, had been trained away. What have they to conceal? What have they to exhibit? Between simple and noble persons there is always a quick intelligence; they recognize at sight, and meet on a better ground than the talents and skills they may chance to possess, namely on sincerity and uprightness. For it is not what talents or genius a man has, but how he is to his talents, that constitutes friendship and character. The man that stands by himself, the universe stands by him also. It is related of the monk Basle, that being excommunicated by the Pope, he was, at his death, sent in charge of an angel to find a fit place of suffering in hell; but such was the eloquence and good-humor of the monk, that wherever he went he was received gladly and civilly treated even by the most uncivil angels; and when he came to discourse with them, instead of contradicting or forcing him, they took his part, and adopted his manners; and even good angels came from far to see him and take up their abode with him. The angel that was sent to find a place of torment for him attempted to remove him to a worse pit, but with no better success; for such was the contented spirit of the monk that he found something to praise in every place and company, though in hell, and made a kind of heaven of it. At last the escorting angel returned with his prisoner to them that sent him, saying that no phlegethon could be found that would burn him; for that in whatever condition, Basle remained incorrigibly Basle. The legend says his sentence was remitted, and he was allowed to go into heaven and was canonized as a saint.

There is a stroke of magnanimity in the correspondence of Bonaparte with his brother Joseph, when the latter was King of Spain, and complained that he missed in Napoleon's letters the affectionate tone which had marked their childish correspondence. " I am sorry," replies Napoleon, " you think you shall find your brother again only in the Elysian Fields. It is natural that at forty he should not feel toward you as he did at twelve. But his feelings toward you have greater truth and strength. His friendship has the features of his mind."

How much we forgive to those who yield us the rare spectacle of heroic manners! We will pardon them the want of books, of arts, and even of the gentler virtues. How tenaciously we remember them! Here is a lesson which I brought along with me in boyhood from the Latin School, and which ranks with the best of Roman anecdotes. Marcus Scaurus was accused by Quintus Varius

Hispanus, that he had excited the allies to take arms against the Republic. But he, full of firmness and gravity, defended himself in this manner : — " Quintus Varius Hispanus alleges that Marcus Scaurus, President of the Senate, excited the allies to arms : Marcus Scaurus, President of the Senate, denies it. There is no witness. Which do you believe, Romans ? " " *Utri creditis, Quirites ?* " When he had said these words he was absolved by the assembly of the people.

I have seen manners that make a similar impression with personal beauty; that give the like exhilaration, and refine us like that; and in memorable experiences they are suddenly better than beauty, and make that superfluous and ugly. But they must be marked by fine perception, the acquaintance with real beauty. They must always show self-control; you shall not be facile, apologetic, or leaky, but king over your word; and every gesture and action shall indicate power at rest. Then they must be inspired by the good heart. There is no beautifier of complexion, or form, or behavior, like the wish to scatter joy and not pain around us. It is good to give a stranger a meal, or a night's lodging. It is better to be hospitable to his good meaning and thought, and give courage to a companion. We must be as courteous to a man as we are to a picture, which we are willing to give the advantage of a good light. Special precepts are not to be thought of; the talent of well-doing contains them all. Every hour will show a duty as paramount as that of my whim just now, and yet I will write it, — that there is one topic peremptorily forbidden to all well-bred, to all rational mortals, namely, their distempers. If you have not slept, or if you have slept, or if you have headache, or sciatica, or leprosy, or thunderstroke, I beseech you by all angels to hold your peace, and not pollute the morning, to which all the housemates bring serene and pleasant thoughts, by corruption and groans. Come out of the azure. Love the day. Do not leave the sky out of your landscape. The oldest and the most deserving person should come very modestly into any newly awaked company, respecting the divine communications out of which all must be presumed to have newly come. An old man who added an elevating culture to a large experience of life, said to me, " When you come into the room, I think I will study how to make humanity beautiful to you."

As respects the delicate question of culture I do not think that any other than negative rules can be laid down. For positive rules, for suggestion, Nature alone inspires it. Who dare assume to guide a youth, a maid, to perfect manners? the golden

mean is so delicate, difficult, — say frankly, unat-
tainable. What finest hands would not be clumsy
to sketch the genial precepts of the young girl's
demeanor ? The chances seem infinite against
success; and yet success is continually attained.
There must not be secondariness, and 't is a thousand to one that her air and manner will at once
betray that she is not primary, but that there is
some other one or many of her class to whom she
habitually postpones herself. But Nature lifts her
easily and without knowing it over these impossi-
bilities, and we are continually surprised with
graces and felicities not only unteachable but undescribable.

VI.

WORSHIP.

———◆———

THIS is he, who, felled by foes,
Sprung harmless up, refreshed by blows:
He to captivity was sold,
But him no prison-bars would hold:
Though they sealed him in a rock,
Mountain chains he can unlock:
Thrown to lions for their meat,
The crouching lion kissed his feet:
Bound to the stake, no flames appalled,
But arched o'er him an honoring vault.
This is he men miscall Fate,
Threading dark ways, arriving late,
But ever coming in time to crown
The truth, and hurl wrongdoers down.
He is the oldest, and best known,
More near than aught thou call'st thy own,
Yet greeted in another's eyes,
Disconcerts with glad surprise.
This is Jove, who, deaf to prayers,
Floods with blessings unawares.
Draw, if thou canst, the mystic line,
Severing rightly his from thine,
Which is human, which divine.

WORSHIP.

Some of my friends have complained, when the preceding papers were read, that we discussed Fate, Power and Wealth on too low a platform; gave too much line to the evil spirit of the times; too many cakes to Cerberus; that we ran Cudworth's risk of making, by excess of candor, the argument of atheism so strong that he could not answer it. I have no fears of being forced in my own despite to play as we say the devil's attorney. I have no infirmity of faith; no belief that it is of much importance what I or any man may say: I am sure that a certain truth will be said through me, though I should be dumb, or though I should try to say the reverse. Nor do I fear skepticism for any good soul. A just thinker will allow full swing to his skepticism. I dip my pen in the blackest ink, because I am not afraid of falling into my inkpot. I have no sympathy with a poor man I knew, who, when suicides abounded, told me he dared not look at his razor. We are of different opinions at different hours, but we always may be said to be at heart on the side of truth.

I see not why we should give ourselves such sanctified airs. If the Divine Providence has hid from men neither disease nor deformity nor corrupt society, but has stated itself out in passions, in war, in trade, in the love of power and pleasure, in hunger and need, in tyrannies, literatures and arts,— let us not be so nice that we cannot write these facts down coarsely as they stand, or doubt but there is a counter-statement as ponderous, which we can arrive at, and which, being put, will make all square. The solar system has no anxiety about its reputation, and the credit of truth and honesty is as safe; nor have I any fear that a skeptical bias can be given by leaning hard on the sides of fate, of practical power, or of trade, which the doctrine of Faith cannot down-weigh. The strength of that principle is not measured in ounces and pounds; it tyrannizes at the centre of Nature. We may well give skepticism as much line as we can. The spirit will return and fill us. It drives the drivers. It counterbalances any accumulations of power : —

"Heaven kindly gave our blood a moral flow."

We are born loyal. The whole creation is made of hooks and eyes, of bitumen, of sticking-plaster; and whether your community is made in Jerusalem or in California, of saints or of wreckers, it coheres in a perfect ball. Men as naturally make a state, or a church, as caterpillars a web. If they were more refined, it would be less formal, it would be nervous, like that of the Shakers, who, from long habit of thinking and feeling together it is said are affected in the same way, at the same time, to work and to play; and as they go with perfect sympathy to their tasks in the field or shop, so are they inclined for a ride or a journey at the same instant, and the horses come up with the family carriage unbespoken to the door.

We are born believing. A man bears beliefs as a tree bears apples. A self-poise belongs to every particle, and a rectitude to every mind, and is the Nemesis and protector of every society. I and my neighbors have been bred in the notion that unless we came soon to some good church, — Calvinism, or Behmenism, or Romanism, or Mormonism, — there would be a universal thaw and dissolution. No Isaiah or Jeremy has arrived. Nothing can exceed the anarchy that has followed in our skies. The stern old faiths have all pulverized. 'T is a whole population of gentlemen and ladies out in search of religions. 'T is as flat anarchy in our ecclesiastic realms as that which existed in Massachusetts in the Revolution, or which prevails now on the slope of the Rocky Mountains or Pike's Peak. Yet we make shift to live. Men are loyal. Nature has self-poise in all her works; certain proportions in which oxygen and azote combine, and not less a harmony in faculties, a fitness in the spring and the regulator. The decline of the influence of Calvin, or Fénelon, or Wesley, or Channing, need give us no uneasiness. The builder of heaven has not so ill constructed his creature as that the religion, that is, the public nature, should fall out: the public and the private element, like north and south, like inside and outside, like centrifugal and centripetal, adhere to every soul, and cannot be subdued except the soul is dissipated. God builds his temple in the heart on the ruins of churches and religions.

In the last chapters we treated some particulars of the question of culture. But the whole state of man is a state of culture; and its flowering and completion may be described as Religion, or Worship. There is always some religion, some hope and fear extended into the invisible, — from the blind boding which nails a horseshoe to the mast or the threshold, up to the song of the Elders in the Apocalypse. But the religion cannot rise above the state of the votary. Heaven always bears some proportion to earth. The god of the cannibals will be a cannibal, of the crusaders a crusader, and of the merchants a merchant. In all ages, souls out of time, extraordinary, prophetic, are born, who are rather related to the system of

the world than to their particular age and locality.
These announce absolute truths, which, with whatever reverence received, are speedily dragged down
into a savage interpretation. The interior tribes of
our Indians and some of the Pacific islanders flog
their gods when things take an unfavorable turn.
The Greek poets did not hesitate to let loose their
petulant wit on their deities also. Laomedon, in his
anger at Neptune and Apollo, who had built Troy
for him and demanded their price, does not hesitate
to menace them that he will cut their ears off.[1]
Among our Norse forefathers, King Olaf's mode of
converting Eyvind to Christianity was to put a pan
of glowing coals on his belly, which burst asunder.
" Wilt thou now, Eyvind, believe in Christ?" asks
Olaf, in excellent faith. Another argument was
an adder put into the mouth of the reluctant dis-
ciple Rand, who refused to believe.

Christianity, in the romantic ages, signified European culture, — the grafted or meliorated tree
in a crab forest. And to marry a pagan wife or
husband was to marry Beast, and voluntarily to
take a step backwards towards the baboon : —

> " Hengist had verament
> A daughter both fair and gent,
> But she was heathen Sarazine,
> And Vortigern for love fine

[1] *Iliad*, Book xxi. l. 455.

> Her took to fere and to wife,
> And was cursed in all his life;
> For he let Christian wed heathen,
> And mixed our blood as flesh and mathen."[1]

What Gothic mixtures the Christian creed drew from the pagan sources, Richard of Devizes' chronicle of Richard I.'s crusade, in the twelfth century, may show.   King Richard taunts God with forsaking him : "O fie! O how unwilling should I be to forsake thee, in so forlorn and dreadful a position, were I thy lord and advocate, as thou art mine.   In sooth, my standards will in future be despised, not through my fault, but through thine : in sooth not through any cowardice of my warfare art thou thyself, my king and my God, conquered this day, and not Richard thy vassal." The religion of the early English poets is anomalous, so devout and so blasphemous, in the same breath.   Such is Chaucer's extraordinary confusion of heaven and earth in the picture of Dido : —

> "She was so fair,
> So young, so lusty, with her eyen glad,
> That if that God that heaven and earthe made
> Would have a love for beauty and goodness,
> And womanhede, truth, and seemliness,
> Whom should he loven but this lady sweet ?
> There n' is no woman to him half so meet."

With these grossnesses, we complacently com-

---

[1] Moths or worms.

pare our own taste and decorum. We think and
speak with more temperance and gradation, — but
is not indifferentism as bad as superstition?

We live in a transition period, when the old
faiths which comforted nations, and not only so
but made nations, seem to have spent their force.
I do not find the religions of men at this moment
very creditable to them, but either childish and
insignificant or unmanly and effeminating. The
fatal trait is the divorce between religion and
morality. Here are know-nothing religions, or
churches that proscribe intellect; scortatory religions; slave-holding and slave-trading religions;
and, even in the decent populations, idolatries
wherein the whiteness of the ritual covers scarlet
indulgence. The lover of the old religion com-
plains that our contemporaries, scholars as well as
merchants, succumb to a great despair, — have corrupted into a timorous conservatism and believe
in nothing. In our large cities the population is
godless, materialized, — no bond, no fellow-feeling,
no enthusiasm. These are not men, but hungers,
thirsts, fevers and appetites walking. How is it
people manage to live on, — so aimless as they
are? After their pepper-corn aims are gained, it
seems as if the lime in their bones alone held
them together, and not any worthy purpose. There
is no faith in the intellectual, none in the moral

universe.   There is faith in chemistry, in meat
and wine, in wealth, in machinery, in the steam-
engine, galvanic battery, turbine-wheels, sewing-
machines, and in public opinion, but not in divine
causes.   A silent revolution has loosed the tension
of the old religious sects, and in place of the gravity and permanence of those societies of opinion,
they run into freak and extravagance.   In creeds
never was such levity ; witness the heathenisms in
Christianity, the periodic " revivals," the Millen-
nium mathematics, the peacock ritualism, the retrogression to Popery, the maundering of Mormons,
the squalor of Mesmerism, the deliration of rap-
pings, the rat and mouse revelation, thumps in
table-drawers, and black art.   The architecture,
the music, the prayer, partake of the madness ; the
arts sink into shift and make-believe.   Not knowing what to do, we ape our ancestors ; the churches
stagger backward to the mummeries of the Dark
Ages.   By the irresistible maturing of the general
mind, the Christian traditions have lost their hold.
The dogma of the mystic offices of Christ being
dropped, and he standing on his genius as a moral
teacher, it is impossible to maintain the old emphasis of his personality ; and it recedes, as all persons must, before the sublimity of the moral laws.
From this change, and in the momentary absence
of any religious genius that could offset the im-

mense material activity, there is a feeling that religion is gone. When Paul Leroux offered his article " Dieu " to the conductor of a leading French journal, he replied, " *La question de Dieu manque d'actualité.*" In Italy, Mr. Gladstone said of the late King of Naples, " It has been a proverb that he has erected the negation of God into a system of government." In this country the like stupefaction was in the air, and the phrase " higher law " became a political jibe. What proof of infidelity like the toleration and propagandism of slavery? What, like the direction of education? What, like the facility of conversion? What, like the externality of churches that once sucked the roots of right and wrong, and now have perished away till they are a speck of whitewash on the wall? What proof of skepticism like the base rate at which the highest mental and moral gifts are held? Let a man attain the highest and broadest culture that any American has possessed, then let him die by sea-storm, railroad collision, or other accident, and all America will acquiesce that the best thing has happened to him; that, after the education has gone far, such is the expensiveness of America that the best use to put a fine person to is to drown him to save his board.

Another scar of this skepticism is the distrust in human virtue. It is believed by well-dressed proprietors that there is no more virtue than they possess; that the solid portion of society exist for the arts of comfort; that life is an affair to put somewhat between the upper and lower mandibles. How prompt the suggestion of a low motive ! Certain patriots in England devoted themselves for years to creating a public opinion that should break down the corn-laws and establish free trade. ' Well,' says the man in the street, ' Cobden got a stipend out of it.' Kossuth fled hither across the ocean to try if he could rouse the New World to a sympathy with European liberty. ' Aye,' says New York, ' he made a handsome thing of it, enough to make him comfortable for life.'

See what allowance vice finds in the respectable and well-conditioned class. If a pickpocket intrude into the society of gentlemen, they exert what moral force they have, and he finds himself uncomfortable and glad to get away. But if an adventurer go through all the forms, procure himself to be elected to a post of trust, as of senator or president, though by the same arts as we detest in the house-thief, — the same gentlemen who agree to discountenance the private rogue will be forward to show civilities and marks of respect to the public one; and no amount of evidence of his crimes will prevent them giving him ovations, complimentary dinners, opening their own houses to him and

priding themselves on his acquaintance. We were
not deceived by the professions of the private adventurer, — the louder he talked of his honor, the
faster we counted our spoons; but we appeal to
the sanctified preamble of the messages and proc-
lamations of the public sinner, as the proof of
sincerity. It must be that they who pay this homage have said to themselves, On the whole, we don't
know about this that you call honesty; a bird in
the hand is better.

Even well-disposed, good sort of people are
touched with the same infidelity, and, for brave,
straightforward action, use half-measures and com-
promises. Forgetful that a little measure is a
great error, forgetful that a wise mechanic uses a
sharp tool, they go on choosing the dead men of
routine. But the official men can in nowise help
you in any question of to-day, they deriving en-
tirely from the old dead things. Only those can
help in counsel or conduct who did not make a
party pledge to defend this or that, but who were
appointed by God Almighty, before they came into
the world, to stand for this which they uphold.

It has been charged that a want of sincerity in
the leading men is a vice general throughout American society. But the multitude of the sick shall
not make us deny the existence of health. In spite
of our imbecility and terrors, and "universal decay

of religion," &c. &c., the moral sense reappears to-
day with the same morning newness that has been
from of old the fountain of beauty and strength.
You say there is no religion now. 'Tis like saying
in rainy weather, There is no sun, when at that
moment we are witnessing one of his superlative
effects. The religion of the cultivated class now,
to be sure, consists in an avoidance of acts and
engagements which it was once their religion to
assume. But this avoidance will yield spontane-
ous forms in their due hour. There is a principle
which is the basis of things, which all speech aims
to say, and all action to evolve, a simple, quiet,
undescribed, undescribable presence, dwelling very
peacefully in us, our rightful lord: we are not to
do, but to let do; not to work, but to be worked
upon; and to this homage there is a consent of all
thoughtful and just men in all ages and conditions.
To this sentiment belong vast and sudden enlarge-
ments of power. 'Tis remarkable that our faith
in ecstasy consists with total inexperience of it. It
is the order of the world to educate with accuracy
the senses and the understanding; and the enginery
at work to draw out these powers in priority, no
doubt has its office. But we are never without a
hint that these powers are mediate and servile, and
that we are one day to deal with real being, — essences with essences. Even the fury of material

activity has some results friendly to moral health. The energetic action of the times develops individualism, and the religious appear isolated. I esteem this a step in the right direction. Heaven deals with us on no representative system. Souls are not saved in bundles. The Spirit saith to the man, 'How is it with thee? thee personally? is it well? is it ill?' For a great nature it is a happiness to escape a religious training, — religion of character is so apt to be invaded. Religion must always be a crab fruit; it cannot be grafted and keep its wild beauty. "I have seen," said a traveller who had known the extremes of society, "I have seen human nature in all its forms; it is everywhere the same, but the wilder it is, the more virtuous."

We say the old forms of religion decay, and that a skepticism devastates the community. I do not think it can be cured or stayed by any modification of theologic creeds, much less by theologic discipline. The cure for false theology is mother-wit. Forget your books and traditions, and obey your moral perceptions at this hour. That which is signified by the words "moral" and "spiritual," is a lasting essence, and, with whatever illusions we have loaded them, will certainly bring back the words, age after age, to their ancient meaning. I know no words that mean so much. In our definitions we grope after the *spiritual* by describing it as invisible. The true meaning of *spiritual* is *real;* that law which executes itself, which works without means, and which cannot be conceived as not existing. Men talk of " mere morality," — which is much as if one should say, 'Poor God, with nobody to help him.' I find the omnipresence and the almightiness in the reaction of every atom in Nature. I can best indicate by examples those reactions by which every part of Nature replies to the purpose of the actor, — beneficently to the good, penally to the bad. Let us replace sentimentalism by realism, and dare to uncover those simple and terrible laws which, be they seen or unseen, pervade and govern.

Every man takes care that his neighbor shall not cheat him. But a day comes when he begins to care that he do not cheat his neighbor. Then all goes well. He has changed his market-cart into a chariot of the sun. What a day dawns when we have taken to heart the doctrine of faith ! to prefer, as a better investment, being to doing; being to seeming; logic to rhythm and to display; the year to the day; the life to the year; character to performance ; — and have come to know that justice will be done us; and if our genius is slow, the term will be long.

It is certain that worship stands in some commanding relation to the health of man and to his highest powers, so as to be in some manner the source of intellect. All the great ages have been ages of belief. I mean, when there was any extraordinary power of performance, when great national movements began, when arts appeared, when heroes existed, when poems were made, — the human soul was in earnest, and had fixed its thoughts on spiritual verities with as strict a grasp as that of the hands on the sword, or the pencil, or the trowel. It is true that genius takes its rise out of the mountains of rectitude; that all beauty and power which men covet are somehow born out of that Alpine district; that any extraordinary degree of beauty in man or woman involves a moral charm. Thus I think we very slowly admit in another man a higher degree of moral sentiment than our own, — a finer conscience, more impressionable or which marks minuter degrees; an ear to hear acuter notes of right and wrong than we can. I think we listen suspiciously and very slowly to any evidence to that point. But, once satisfied of such superiority, we set no limit to our expectation of his genius. For such persons are nearer to the secret of God than others; are bathed by sweeter waters; they hear notices, they see visions, where others are vacant. We believe that holiness confers a certain insight, because not by our private but by our public force can we share and know the nature of things.

There is an intimate interdependence of intellect
and morals. Given the equality of two intellects,
— which will form the most reliable judgments,
the good, or the bad hearted ? " The heart has its
arguments, with which the understanding is not
acquainted." For the heart is at once aware of the
state of health or disease, which is the controlling
state, that is, — of sanity or of insanity ; prior of
course to all question of the ingenuity of arguments, the amount of facts, or the elegance of rhetoric. So intimate is this alliance of mind and
heart, that talent uniformly sinks with character.
The bias of errors of principle carries away men
into perilous courses as soon as their will does not
control their passion or talent. Hence the extraordinary blunders and final wrong head into which
men spoiled by ambition usually fall. Hence the
remedy for all blunders, the cure of blindness, the
cure of crime, is love. " As much love, so much
mind," said the Latin proverb. The superiority
that has no superior ; the redeemer and instructor
of souls, as it is their primal essence, is love.

The moral must be the measure of health. If
your eye is on the eternal, your intellect will grow,
and your opinions and actions will have a beauty
which no learning or combined advantages of other
men can rival. The moment of your loss of faith
and acceptance of the lucrative standard will be

marked in the pause or solstice of genius, the sequent retrogression, and the inevitable loss of attraction to other minds. The vulgar are sensible of the change in you, and of your descent, though they clap you on the back and congratulate you on your increased common-sense.

Our recent culture has been in natural science. We have learned the manners of the sun and of the moon, of the rivers and the rain, of the mineral and elemental kingdoms, of plants and animals. Man has learned to weigh the sun, and its weight neither loses nor gains. The path of a star, the moment of an eclipse, can be determined to the fraction of a second. Well, to him the book of history, the book of love, the lures of passion and the commandments of duty are opened; and the next lesson taught is the continuation of the inflexible law of matter into the subtile kingdom of will and of thought; that if in sidereal ages gravity and projection keep their craft, and the ball never loses its way in its wild path through space, — a secreter gravitation, a secreter projection rule not less tyrannically in human history, and keep the balance of power from age to age unbroken. For though the new element of freedom and an individual has been admitted, yet the primordial atoms are prefigured and predetermined to moral issues, are in search of justice, and ultimate right is done.

Religion or worship is the attitude of those who see this unity, intimacy, and sincerity; who see that against all appearances the nature of things works for truth and right forever.

It is a short sight to limit our faith in laws to those of gravity, of chemistry, of botany, and so forth. Those laws do not stop where our eyes lose them, but push the same geometry and chemistry up into the invisible plane of social and rational life, so that look where we will, in a boy's game, or in the strifes of races, a perfect reaction, a perpetual judgment keeps watch and ward. And this appears in a class of facts which concerns all men, within and above their creeds.

Shallow men believe in luck, believe in circumstances: it was somebody's name, or he happened to be there at the time, or it was so then and another day it would have been otherwise. Strong men believe in cause and effect. The man was born to do it, and his father was born to be the father of him and of his deed; and by looking narrowly you shall see there was no luck in the matter; but it was all a problem in arithmetic, or an experiment in chemistry. The curve of the flight of the moth is preordained, and all things go by number, rule, and weight.

Skepticism is unbelief in cause and effect. A man does not see that as he eats, so he thinks; as he deals, so he is, and so he appears; he does not see that his son is the son of his thoughts and of his actions; that fortunes are not exceptions but fruits; that relation and connection are not somewhere and sometimes, but everywhere and always; no miscellany, no exemption, no anomaly, — but method, and an even web; and what comes out, that was put in. As we are, so we do; and as we do, so is it done to us; we are the builders of our fortunes; cant and lying and the attempt to secure a good which does not belong to us, are, once for all, balked and vain. But, in the human mind, this tie of fate is made alive. The law is the basis of the human mind. In us, it is inspiration; out there in Nature we see its fatal strength. We call it the moral sentiment.

We owe to the Hindoo Scriptures a definition of Law, which compares well with any in our Western books. "Law it is, which is without name, or color, or hands, or feet; which is smallest of the least, and largest of the large; all, and knowing all things; which hears without ears, sees without eyes, moves without feet, and seizes without hands."

If any reader tax me with using vague and traditional phrases, let me suggest to him by a few examples what kind of a trust this is, and how real. Let me show him that the dice are loaded; that the colors are fast, because they are the native colors of the fleece; that the globe is a battery, because every atom is a magnet; and that the police and sincerity of the Universe are secured by God's delegating his divinity to every particle; that there is no room for hypocrisy, no margin for choice.

The countryman leaving his native village for the first time and going abroad, finds all his habits broken up. In a new nation and language, his sect, as Quaker, or Lutheran, is lost. What! it is not then necessary to the order and existence of society? He misses this, and the commanding eye of his neighborhood, which held him to decorum. This is the peril of New York, of New Orleans, of London, of Paris, to young men. But after a little experience he makes the discovery that there are no large cities, — none large enough to hide in; that the censors of action are as numerous and as near in Paris, as in Littleton or Portland; that the gossip is as prompt and vengeful. There is no concealment, and for each offence a several vengeance; that reaction, or *nothing for nothing*, or, *things are as broad as they are long*, is not a rule for Littleton or Portland, but for the Universe.

We cannot spare the coarsest muniment of virtue. We are disgusted by gossip, yet it is of importance to keep the angels in their proprieties. The smallest fly will draw blood, and gossip is a

weapon impossible to exclude from the privatest,
highest, selectest. Nature created a police of many
ranks. God has delegated himself to a million dep-
uties. From these low external penalties the scale
ascends. Next come the resentments, the fears,
which injustice calls out; then the false relations
in which the offender is put to other men; and the
reaction of his fault on himself, in the solitude and
devastation of his mind.

You cannot hide any secret. If the artist succor
his flagging spirits by opium or wine, his work will
characterize itself as the effect of opium or wine.
If you make a picture or a statue, it sets the beholder in that state of mind you had when you
made it. If you spend for show, on building, or
gardening, or on pictures, or on equipages, it will
so appear. We are all physiognomists and pene-
trators of character, and things themselves are de-
tective. If you follow the suburban fashion in
building a sumptuous-looking house for a little
money, it will appear to all eyes as a cheap dear
house. There is no privacy that cannot be pene-
trated. No secret can be kept in the civilized
world. Society is a masked ball, where every one
hides his real character, and reveals it by hiding.
If a man wish to conceal anything he carries, those
whom he meets know that he conceals somewhat,
and usually know what he conceals. Is it other-

wise if there be some belief or some purpose he
would bury in his breast? 'T is as hard to hide as
fire. He is a strong man who can hold down his
opinion. A man cannot utter two or three sentences without disclosing to intelligent ears precisely where he stands in life and thought, namely,
whether in the kingdom of the senses and the understanding, or in that of ideas and imagination,
in the realm of intuitions and duty. People seem
not to see that their opinion of the world is also a
confession of character. We can only see what we
are, and if we misbehave we suspect others. The
fame of Shakspeare or of Voltaire, of Thomas à
Kempis or of Bonaparte, characterizes those who
give it. As gas-light is found to be the best noc-
turnal police, so the universe protects itself by piti-
less publicity.

Each must be armed — not necessarily with mus-
ket and pike. Happy, if, seeing these, he can feel
that he has better muskets and pikes in his energy and constancy. To every creature is his own
weapon, however skilfully concealed from himself,
a good while. His work is sword and shield.
Let him accuse none, let him injure none. The
way to mend the bad world is to create the right
world. Here is a low political economy plotting to
cut the throat of foreign competition and establish
our own ; excluding others by force, or making

war on them ; or by cunning tariffs giving prefer-
ence to worse wares of ours. But the real and
lasting victories are those of peace and not of war.
The way to conquer the foreign artisan is, not to
kill him, but to beat his work. And the Crystal
Palaces and World Fairs, with their committees
and prizes on all kinds of industry, are the result of this feeling. The American workman who
strikes ten blows with his hammer whilst the foreign workman only strikes one, is as really van-
quishing that foreigner as if the blows were aimed
at and told on his person. I look on that man
as happy, who, when there is question of success,
looks into his work for a reply, not into the market,
not into opinion, not into patronage. In every variety of human employment, in the mechanical and
in the fine arts, in navigation, in farming, in legis-
lating, there are, among the numbers who do their
task perfunctorily, as we say, or just to pass, and
as badly as they dare, — there are the working-
men, on whom the burden of the business falls ;
those who love work, and love to see it rightly
done ; who finish their task for its own sake ; and
the state and the world is happy that has the most
of such finishers. The world will always do justice
at last to such finishers ; it cannot otherwise. He
who has acquired the ability may wait securely the
occasion of making it felt and appreciated, and

know that it will not loiter. Men talk as if victory were something fortunate. Work is victory. Wherever work is done, victory is obtained. There is no chance, and no blanks. You want but one verdict; if you have your own you are secure of the rest. And yet, if witnesses are wanted, witnesses are near. There was never a man born so wise or good but one or more companions came into the world with him, who delight in his faculty and report it. I cannot see without awe that no man thinks alone and no man acts alone, but the divine assessors who came up with him into life, — now under one disguise, now under another, like a police in citizens' clothes, — walk with him, step for step, through all the kingdom of time.

This reaction, this sincerity is the property of all things. To make our word or act sublime, we must make it real. It is our system that counts, not the single word or unsupported action. Use what language you will, you can never say anything but what you are. What I am and what I think is conveyed to you, in spite of my efforts to hold it back. What I am has been secretly conveyed from me to another, whilst I was vainly making up my mind to tell him it. He has heard from me what I never spoke.

As men get on in life, they acquire a love for sincerity, and somewhat less solicitude to be lulled or amused. In the progress of the character, there is an increasing faith in the moral sentiment, and a decreasing faith in propositions. Young people admire talents and particular excellences. As we grow older we value total powers and effects, as the spirit or quality of the man. We have another sight, and a new standard; an insight which disregards what is done *for* the eye, and pierces to the doer; an ear which hears not what men say, but hears what they do not say.

There was a wise, devout man who is called, in the Catholic Church, St. Philip Neri, of whom many anecdotes touching his discernment and benevolence are told at Naples and Rome. Among the nuns in a convent not far from Rome, one had appeared who laid claim to certain rare gifts of inspiration and prophecy, and the abbess advised the Holy Father at Rome of the wonderful powers shown by her novice. The Pope did not well know what to make of these new claims, and Philip coming in from a journey one day, he consulted him. Philip undertook to visit the nun and ascertain her character. He threw himself on his mule, all travel-soiled as he was, and hastened through the mud and mire to the distant convent. He told the abbess the wishes of his Holiness, and begged her to summon the nun without delay. The nun was sent for, and as soon as she came into the apart-

ment, Philip stretched out his leg, all bespattered
with mud, and desired her to draw off his boots.
The young nun, who had become the object of much
attention and respect, drew back with anger, and
refused the office : Philip ran out of doors, mounted
his mule and returned instantly to the Pope ;
" Give yourself no uneasiness, Holy Father, any
longer: here is no miracle, for here is no humility."

We need not much mind what people please to
say, but what they must say; what their natures
say, though their busy, artful, Yankee understand-
ings try to hold back and choke that word, and
to articulate something different. If we will sit
quietly, what they ought to say is said, with their
will or against their will. We do not care for
you, let us pretend what we may : — we are always
looking through you to the dim dictator behind you.
Whilst your habit or whim chatters, we civilly and
impatiently wait until that wise superior shall speak
again. Even children are not deceived by the false
reasons which their parents give in answer to their
questions, whether touching natural facts, or religion, or persons. When the parent, instead of
thinking how it really is, puts them off with a
traditional or a hypocritical answer, the children
perceive that it is traditional or hypocritical. To a
sound constitution the defect of another is at once
manifest; and the marks of it are only concealed

from us by our own dislocation. An anatomical
observer remarks that the sympathies of the chest,
abdomen, and pelvis, tell at last on the face, and
on all its features. Not only does our beauty
waste, but it leaves word how it went to waste.
Physiognomy and phrenology are not new sciences,
but declarations of the soul that it is aware of
certain new sources of information. And now
sciences of broader scope are starting up behind
these. And so for ourselves it is really of little
importance what blunders in statement we make,
so only we make no wilful departures from the
truth. How a man's truth comes to mind, long
after we have forgotten all his words! How it
comes to us in silent hours, that truth is our only
armor in all passages of life and death! Wit is
cheap, and anger is cheap; but if you cannot argue
or explain yourself to the other party, cleave to
the truth, against me against thee, and you gain a
station from which you cannot be dislodged. The
other party will forget the words that you spoke,
but the part you took continues to plead for you.

Why should I hasten to solve every riddle which
life offers me? I am well assured that the Ques-
tioner who brings me so many problems will bring
the answers also in due time. Very rich, very potent, very cheerful Giver that he is, he shall have it
all his own way, for me. Why should I give up

my thought, because I cannot answer an objection
to it? Consider only whether it remains in my
life the same it was. That only which we have
within, can we see without. If we meet no gods,
it is because we harbor none. If there is grandeur in you, you will find grandeur in porters and
sweeps. He only is rightly immortal to whom all
things are immortal. I have read somewhere that
none is accomplished so long as any are incom-
plete; that the happiness of one cannot consist with
the misery of any other.

The Buddhists say, "No seed will die:" every
seed will grow. Where is the service which can
escape its remuneration? What is vulgar, and the
essence of all vulgarity, but the avarice of reward?
'T is the difference of artisan and artist, of talent
and genius, of sinner and saint. The man whose
eyes are nailed, not on the nature of his act but on
the wages, whether it be money, or office, or fame,
is almost equally low. He is great whose eyes are
opened to see that the reward of actions cannot be
escaped, because he is transformed into his action,
and taketh its nature, which bears its own fruit,
like every other tree. A great man cannot be hin-
dered of the effect of his act, because it is immedi-
ate. The genius of life is friendly to the noble,
and in the dark brings them friends from far.
Fear God, and where you go, men shall think they
walk in hallowed cathedrals.

And so I look on those sentiments which make the glory of the human being, love, humility, faith, as being also the intimacy of Divinity in the atoms; and that as soon as the man is right, assurances and previsions emanate from the interior of his body and his mind; as, when flowers reach their ripeness, incense exhales from them, and as a beautiful atmosphere is generated from the planet by the averaged emanations from all its rocks and soils.

Thus man is made equal to every event. He can face danger for the right. A poor, tender, painful body, he can run into flame or bullets or pestilence, with duty for his guide. He feels the insurance of a just employment. I am not afraid of accident as long as I am in my place. It is strange that superior persons should not feel that they have some better resistance against cholera than avoiding green peas and salads. Life is hardly respectable, — is it? if it has no generous, guaranteeing task, no duties or affections that constitute a necessity of existing. Every man's task is his life-preserver. The conviction that his work is dear to God and cannot be spared, defends him. The lightning-rod that disarms the cloud of its threat is his body in its duty. A high aim reacts on the means, on the days, on the organs of the body. A high aim is curative, as well as arnica.

" Napoleon," says Goethe, " visited those sick of the plague, in order to prove that the man who could vanquish fear could vanquish the plague also; and he was right. It is incredible what force the will has in such cases: it penetrates the body and puts it in a state of activity which repels all hurtful influences; whilst fear invites them."

It is related of William of Orange, that whilst he was besieging a town on the continent, a gentleman sent to him on public business came to his camp, and, learning that the King was before the walls, he ventured to go where he was. He found him directing the operation of his gunners, and having explained his errand and received his answer, the King said, " Do you not know, sir, that every moment you spend here is at the risk of your life?" " I run no more risk," replied the gentleman, " than your Majesty." " Yes," said the King, " but my duty brings me here, and yours does not." In a few minutes a cannon-ball fell on the spot, and the gentleman was killed.

Thus can the faithful student reverse all the warnings of his early instinct, under the guidance of a deeper instinct. He learns to welcome misfortune, learns that adversity is the prosperity of the great. He learns the greatness of humility. He shall work in the dark, work against failure, pain, and ill-will. If he is insulted, he can be insulted ; all his affair is not to insult. Hafiz writes, —

> "At the last day, men shall wear
> On their heads the dust,
> As ensign and as ornament
> Of their lowly trust."

The moral equalizes all ; enriches, empowers all. It is the coin which buys all, and which all find in their pocket. Under the whip of the driver, the slave shall feel his equality with saints and heroes. In the greatest destitution and calamity it surprises man with a feeling of elasticity which makes nothing of loss.

I recall some traits of a remarkable person whose life and discourse betrayed many inspirations of this sentiment. Benedict was always great in the present time. He had hoarded nothing from the past, neither in his cabinets, neither in his memory. He had no designs on the future, neither for what he should do to men, nor for what men should do for him. He said, " I am never beaten until I know that I am beaten. I meet powerful brutal people to whom I have no skill to reply. They think they have defeated me. It is so published in society, in the journals ; I am defeated in this fashion, in all men's sight, perhaps on a dozen different lines. My ledger may show that I am in debt, cannot yet make

my ends meet and vanquish the enemy so. My
race may not be prospering ; we are sick, ugly,
obscure, unpopular. My children may be worsted.
I seem to fail in my friends and clients, too. That
is to say, in all the encounters that have yet
chanced, I have not been weaponed for that particular occasion, and have been historically beaten ;
and yet I know all the time that I have never
been beaten ; have never yet fought, shall certainly
fight when my hour comes, and shall beat." " A
man," says the Vishnu Sarma, " who having well
compared his own strength or weakness with that
of others, after all doth not know the difference, is
easily overcome by his enemies."

" I spent," he said, " ten months in the country. Thick-starred Orion was my only companion.
Wherever a squirrel or a bee can go with security,
I can go. I ate whatever was set before me ; I
touched ivy and dogwood. When I went abroad,
I kept company with every man on the road, for I
knew that my evil and my good did not come from
these, but from the Spirit, whose servant I was.
For I could not stoop to be a circumstance, as they
did who put their life into their fortune and their
company. I would not degrade myself by casting
about in my memory for a thought, nor by waiting
for one. If the thought come, I would give it
entertainment. It should, as it ought, go into my

hands and feet; but if it come not spontaneously, it comes not rightly at all. If it can spare me, I am sure I can spare it. It shall be the same with my friends. I will never woo the loveliest. I will not ask any friendship or favor. When I come to my own, we shall both know it. Nothing will be to be asked or to be granted." Benedict went out to seek his friend, and met him on the way; but he expressed no surprise at any coincidences. On the other hand, if he called at the door of his friend and he was not at home, he did not go again; concluding that he had misinterpreted the intimations.

He had the whim not to make an apology to the same individual whom he had wronged. For this he said was a piece of personal vanity; but he would correct his conduct, in that respect in which he had faulted, to the next person he should meet. Thus, he said, universal justice was satisfied.

Mira came to ask what she should do with the poor Genesee woman who had hired herself to work for her, at a shilling a day, and, now sickening, was like to be bedridden on her hands. Should she keep her, or should she dismiss her? But Benedict said, "Why ask? One thing will clear itself as the thing to be done, and not another, when the hour comes. Is it a question whether to put her into the street? Just as much whether to thrust the little Jenny on your arm into the street. The milk and meal you give the beggar will fatten Jenny. Thrust the woman out, and you thrust your babe out of doors, whether it so seem to you or not."

In the Shakers, so called, I find one piece of belief, in the doctrine which they faithfully hold that encourages them to open their doors to every wayfaring man who proposes to come among them; for, they say, the Spirit will presently manifest to the man himself and to the society what manner of person he is, and whether he belongs among them. They do not receive him, they do not reject him. And not in vain have they worn their clay coat, and drudged in their fields, and shuffled in their Bruin dance, from year to year, if they have truly learned thus much wisdom.

Honor him whose life is perpetual victory; him who, by sympathy with the invisible and real, finds support in labor, instead of praise ; who does not shine, and would rather not. With eyes open, he makes the choice of virtue which outrages the virtuous ; of religion which churches stop their discords to burn and exterminate ; for the highest virtue is always against the law.

Miracle comes to the miraculous, not to the arithmetician. Talent and success interest me but moderately. The great class, they who affect our imagination, the men who could not make their hands meet around their objects, the rapt, the lost, the fools of ideas, — they suggest what they cannot execute. They speak to the ages, and are heard from afar. The Spirit does not love cripples and malformations. If there ever was a good man, be certain there was another and will be more.

And so in relation to that future hour, that spectre clothed with beauty at our curtain by night, at our table by day, — the apprehension, the assurance of a coming change. The race of mankind have always offered at least this implied thanks for the gift of existence, — namely, the terror of its being taken away; the insatiable curiosity and appetite for its continuation. The whole revelation that is vouchsafed us is the gentle trust, which, in our experience we find will cover also with flowers the slopes of this chasm.

Of immortality, the soul when well employed is incurious. It is so well, that it is sure it will be well. It asks no questions of the Supreme Power. The son of Antiochus asked his father when he would join battle? " Dost thou fear," replied the King, " that thou only in all the army wilt not hear the trumpet ? " 'T is a higher thing to confide that if it is best we should live, we shall live, — 't is higher to have this conviction, than to have the lease of indefinite centuries and millenniums and

æons.   Higher than the question of our duration is
the question of our deserving.   Immortality will
come to such as are fit for it, and he who would be
a great soul in future, must be a great soul now.
It is a doctrine too great to rest on any legend, that
is, on any man's experience but our own.   It must
be proved, if at all, from our own activity and
designs, which imply an interminable future for
their play.

What is called religion effeminates and demoralizes.   Such as you are, the gods themselves could
not help you.   Men are too often unfit to live, from
their obvious inequality to their own necessities; or
they suffer from politics, or bad neighbors, or from
sickness, and they would gladly know that they
were to be dismissed from the duties of life.   But
the wise instinct asks, 'How will death help them?'
These are not dismissed when they die.   You shall
not wish for death out of pusillanimity.   The weight
of the Universe is pressed down on the shoulders of
each moral agent to hold him to his task.   The
only path of escape known in all the worlds of God
is performance.   You must do your work, before
you shall be released.   And as far as it is a question of fact respecting the government of the Universe, Marcus Antoninus summed the whole in a
word, "It is pleasant to die if there be gods, and
sad to live if there be none."

And so I think that the last lesson of life, the choral song which rises from all elements and all angels, is a voluntary obedience, a necessitated freedom. Man is made of the same atoms as the world is, he shares the same impressions, predispositions, and destiny. When his mind is illuminated, when his heart is kind, he throws himself joyfully into the sublime order, and does, with knowledge, what the stones do by structure.

The religion which is to guide and fulfil the present and coming ages, whatever else it be, must be intellectual. The scientific mind must have a faith which is science. " There are two things," said Mahomet, " which I abhor, the learned in his infidelities, and the fool in his devotions." Our times are impatient of both, and specially of the last. Let us have nothing now which is not its own evidence. There is surely enough for the heart and imagination in the religion itself. Let us not be pestered with assertions and half-truths, with emotions and snuffle.

There will be a new church founded on moral science; at first cold and naked, a babe in a manger again, the algebra and mathematics of ethical law, the church of men to come, without shawms, or psaltery, or sackbut; but it will have heaven and earth for its beams and rafters; science for symbol and illustration; it will fast enough gather beauty, music, picture, poetry. Was never stoicism so stern and exigent as this shall be. It shall send man home to his central solitude, shame these social, supplicating manners, and make him know that much of the time he must have himself to his friend. He shall expect no co-operation, he shall walk with no companion. The nameless Thought, the nameless Power, the super-personal Heart, — he shall repose alone on that. He needs only his own verdict. No good fame can help, no bad fame can hurt him. The Laws are his consolers, the good Laws themselves are alive, they know if he have kept them, they animate him with the leading of great duty, and an endless horizon. Honor and fortune exist to him who always recognizes the neighborhood of the great, — always feels himself in the presence of high causes.

VII.

CONSIDERATIONS BY THE WAY.

———◆———

Hear what British Merlin sung,
Of keenest eye and truest tongue.
Say not, the chiefs who first arrive
Usurp the seats for which all strive;
The forefathers this land who found
Failed to plant the vantage-ground;
Ever from one who comes to-morrow
Men wait their good and truth to borrow.
But wilt thou measure all thy road,
See thou lift the lightest load.
Who has little, to him who has less, can spare,
And thou, Cyndyllan's son! beware
Ponderous gold and stuffs to bear,
To falter ere thou thy task fulfil, —
Only the light-armed climb the hill.
The richest of all lords is Use,
And ruddy Health the loftiest Muse.
Live in the sunshine, swim the sea,
Drink the wild air's salubrity:
Where the star Canope shines in May,
Shepherds are thankful, and nations gay.

The music that can deepest reach,
And cure all ill, is cordial speech:
Mask thy wisdom with delight,
Toy with the bow, yet hit the white.
Of all wit's uses, the main one
Is to live well with who has none.
Cleave to thine acre; the round year
Will fetch all fruits and virtues here:
Fool and foe may harmless roam,
Loved and lovers bide at home.
A day for toil, an hour for sport,
But for a friend is life too short.

CONSIDERATIONS BY THE WAY.

ALTHOUGH this garrulity of advising is born with us, I confess that life is rather a subject of wonder than of didactics. So much fate, so much irresistible dictation from temperament and unknown inspiration enters into it, that we doubt we can say anything out of our own experience whereby to help each other. All the professions are timid and expectant agencies. The priest is glad if his prayers or his sermon meet the condition of any soul; if of two, if of ten, 'tis a signal success. But he walked to the church without any assurance that he knew the distemper, or could heal it. The physician prescribes hesitatingly out of his few resources the same tonic or sedative to this new and peculiar constitution which he has applied with various success to a hundred men before. If the patient mends he is glad and surprised. The lawyer advises the client, and tells his story to the jury and leaves it with them, and is as gay and as much relieved as the client if it turns out that he has a verdict. The judge weighs the arguments and puts a brave face on the matter, and, since there must be a decision, decides as he can, and hopes he has done justice and given satisfaction to the community; but is only an advocate after all. And so is all life a timid and unskilful spectator. We do what we must, and call it by the best names. We like very well to be praised for our action, but our conscience says, "Not unto us." 'T is little we can do for each other. We accompany the youth with sympathy and manifold old sayings of the wise to the gate of the arena, but 't is certain that not by strength of ours, or of the old sayings, but only on strength of his own, unknown to us or to any, he must stand or fall. That by which a man conquers in any passage is a profound secret to every other being in the world, and it is only as he turns his back on us and on all men and draws on this most private wisdom, that any good can come to him. What we have therefore to say of life, is rather description, or if you please, celebration, than available rules.

Yet vigor is contagious, and whatever makes us either think or feel strongly, adds to our power and enlarges our field of action. We have a debt to every great heart, to every fine genius; to those who have put life and fortune on the cast of an act of justice; to those who have added new sciences; to those who have refined life by elegant pursuits. 'T is the fine souls who serve us, and

not what is called fine society. Fine society is
only a self-protection against the vulgarities of the
street and the tavern. Fine society, in the common
acceptation, has neither ideas nor aims. It renders the service of a perfumery or a laundry, not
of a farm or factory. 'Tis an exclusion and a
precinct. Sydney Smith said, "A few yards in
London cement or dissolve friendship." It is an
unprincipled decorum; an affair of clean linen and
coaches, of gloves, cards, and elegance in trifles.
There are other measures of self-respect for a man
than the number of clean shirts he puts on every
day. Society wishes to be amused. I do not wish
to be amused. I wish that life should not be cheap,
but sacred. I wish the days to be as centuries,
loaded, fragrant. Now we reckon them as bank-
days, by some debt which is to be paid us or which
we are to pay, or some pleasure we are to taste.
Is all we have to do to draw the breath in and
blow it out again? Porphyry's definition is better; "Life is that which holds matter together."
The babe in arms is a channel through which the
energies we call fate, love and reason, visibly stream.
See what a cometary train of auxiliaries man carries with him, of animals, plants, stones, gases and
imponderable elements. Let us infer his ends
from this pomp of means. Mirabeau said, "Why
should we feel ourselves to be men, unless it be to

succeed in everything, everywhere. You must say
of nothing, *That is beneath me*, nor feel that anything can be out of your power. Nothing is impossible to the man who can will. *Is that necessary? That shall be:* — this is the only law of
success." Whoever said it, this is in the right
key. But this is not the tone and genius of the
men in the street. In the streets we grow cynical.
The men we meet are coarse and torpid. The
finest wits have their sediment. What quantities
of fribbles, paupers, invalids, epicures, antiquaries,
politicians, thieves, and triflers of both sexes, might
be advantageously spared! Mankind divides itself into two classes, — benefactors and malefac-
tors. The second class is vast, the first a handful.
A person seldom falls sick but the bystanders are
animated with a faint hope that he will die: —
quantities of poor lives, of distressing invalids, of
cases for a gun. Franklin said, " Mankind are
very superficial and dastardly : they begin upon a
thing, but, meeting with a difficulty, they fly from
it discouraged ; but they have capacities, if they
would employ them." Shall we then judge a country by the majority, or by the minority? By the
minority, surely. 'T is pedantry to estimate nations by the census, or by square miles of land, or
other than by their importance to the mind of the
time.

Leave this hypocritical prating about the masses. Masses are rude, lame, unmade, pernicious in their demands and influence, and need not to be flattered but to be schooled. I wish not to concede anything to them, but to tame, drill, divide and break them up, and draw individuals out of them. The worst of charity is that the lives you are asked to preserve are not worth preserving. Masses! the calamity is the masses. I do not wish any mass at all, but honest men only, lovely, sweet, accomplished women only, and no shovel-handed, narrow-brained, gin-drinking million stockingers or lazzaroni at all. If government knew how, I should like to see it check, not multiply the population. When it reaches its true law of action, every man that is born will be hailed as essential. Away with this hurrah of masses, and let us have the considerate vote of single men spoken on their honor and their conscience. In old Egypt it was established law that the vote of a prophet be reckoned equal to a hundred hands. I think it was much under-estimated. "Clay and clay differ in dignity," as we discover by our preferences every day. What a vicious practice is this of our politicians at Washington pairing off! as if one man who votes wrong going away, could excuse you, who mean to vote right, for going away; or as if your presence did not tell in more ways than in your vote. Suppose the three hundred heroes at Thermopylæ had paired off with three hundred Persians ; would it have been all the same to Greece, and to history ? Napoleon was called by his men *Cent Mille.* Add honesty to him, and they might have called him Hundred Million.

Nature makes fifty poor melons for one that is good, and shakes down a tree full of gnarled, wormy, unripe crabs, before you can find a dozen dessert apples ; and she scatters nations of naked Indians and nations of clothed Christians, with two or three good heads among them. Nature works very hard, and only hits the white once in a million throws. In mankind she is contented if she yields one master in a century. The more difficulty there is in creating good men, the more they are used when they come. I once counted in a little neighborhood and found that every able-bodied man had say from twelve to fifteen persons dependent on him for material aid, — to whom he is to be for spoon and jug, for backer and sponsor, for nursery and hospital and many functions beside : nor does it seem to make much difference whether he is bachelor or patriarch ; if he do not violently decline the duties that fall to him, this amount of helpfulness will in one way or another be brought home to him. This is the tax which his abilities pay. The good men are employed for private cen-

tres of use, and for larger influence. All revelations, whether of mechanical or intellectual or
moral science, are made, not to communities but to
single persons. All the marked events of our day,
all the cities, all the colonizations, may be traced
back to their origin in a private brain. All the
feats which make our civility were the thoughts of
a few good heads.

Meantime this spawning productivity is not nox-
ious or needless. You would say this rabble of
nations might be spared. But no, they are all
counted and depended on. Fate keeps everything
alive so long as the smallest thread of public necessity holds it on to the tree. The coxcomb and
bully and thief class are allowed as proletaries,
every one of their vices being the excess or acridity
of a virtue. The mass are animal, in pupilage, and
near chimpanzee. But the units whereof this mass
is composed, are neuters, every one of which may
be grown to a queen-bee. The rule is, we are used
as brute atoms until we think: then we use all the
rest. Nature turns all malfeasance to good. Nature provided for real needs. No sane man at last
distrusts himself. His existence is a perfect answer to all sentimental cavils. If he is, he is
wanted, and has the precise properties that are
required. That we are here, is proof we ought
to be here. We have as good right, and the same

sort of right to be here, as Cape Cod or Sandy Hook have to be there.

To say then, the majority are wicked, means no malice, no bad heart in the observer, but simply that the majority are unripe, and have not yet come to themselves, do not yet know their opinion. *That*, if they knew it, is an oracle for them and for all. But in the passing moment the quadruped interest is very prone to prevail; and this beast-force, whilst it makes the discipline of the world, the school of heroes, the glory of martyrs, has provoked in every age the satire of wits and the tears of good men. They find the journals, the clubs, the governments, the churches, to be in the interest and the pay of the devil. And wise men have met this obstruction in their times, like Socrates, with his famous irony; like Bacon, with life-long dissimulation; like Erasmus, with his book "The Praise of Folly;" like Rabelais, with his satire rending the nations. "They were the fools who cried against me, you will say," wrote the Chevalier de Boufflers to Grimm; " aye, but the fools have the advantage of numbers, and 't is that which decides. It is of no use for us to make war with them; we shall not weaken them; they will always be the masters. There will not be a practice or an usage introduced, of which they are not the authors."

In front of these sinister facts, the first lesson of

history is the good of evil. Good is a good doctor but Bad is sometimes a better. The oppressions of William the Norman, savage forest - laws and crushing despotism made possible the inspirations of *Magna Charta* under John. Edward I. wanted money, armies, castles, and as much as he could get. It was necessary to call the people together by shorter, swifter ways, — and the House of Commons arose. To obtain subsidies, he paid in privileges. In the twenty-fourth year of his reign he decreed " that no tax should be levied without consent of Lords and Commons ; " — which is the basis of the English Constitution. Plutarch affirms that the cruel wars which followed the march of Alexander introduced the civility, language, and arts of Greece into the savage East; introduced marriage ; built seventy cities, and united hostile nations under one government. The barbarians who broke up the Roman empire did not arrive a day too soon. Schiller says the Thirty Years' War made Germany a nation. Rough, selfish despots serve men immensely, as Henry VIII. in the contest with the Pope ; as the infatuations no less than the wisdom of Cromwell ; as the ferocity of the Russian czars ; as the fanaticism of the French regicides of 1789. The frost which kills the harvest of a year, saves the harvests of a century, by destroying the weevil or the locust. Wars, fires,

plagues, break up immovable routine, clear the
ground of rotten races and dens of distemper, and
open a fair field to new men.   There is a tendency
in things to right themselves, and the war or revolution or bankruptcy that shatters a rotten system,
allows things to take a new and natural order.   The
sharpest evils are bent into that periodicity which
makes the errors of planets and the fevers and distempers of men, self-limiting.   Nature is upheld by
antagonism.   Passions, resistance, danger, are educators.   We acquire the strength we have overcome.
Without war, no soldiers ; without enemies, no hero.
The sun were insipid, if the universe were not
opaque.   And the glory of character is in affront-
ing the horrors of depravity to draw thence new
nobilities of power; as Art lives and thrills in new
use and combining of contrasts, and mining into
the dark evermore for blacker pits of night.   What
would painter do, or what would poet or saint, but
for crucifixions and hells?   And evermore in the
world is this marvellous balance of beauty and disgust, magnificence and rats.   Not Antoninus, but a
poor washer-woman said, " The more trouble, the
more lion ; that 's my principle."

I do not think very respectfully of the designs or
the doings of the people who went to California in
1849.   It was a rush and a scramble of needy ad-
venturers, and, in the western country, a general

jail-delivery of all the rowdies of the rivers. Some of them went with honest purposes, some with very bad ones, and all of them with the very common-place wish to find a short way to wealth. But Nature watches over all, and turns this malfeasance to good. California gets peopled and subdued, civilized in this immoral way, and on this fiction a real prosperity is rooted and grown. 'T is a de-coy-duck; 't is tubs thrown to amuse the whale ; but real ducks, and whales that yield oil, are caught. And out of Sabine rapes, and out of robbers' forays, real Romes and their heroisms come in fulness of time.

In America the geography is sublime but the men are not : the inventions are excellent but the inventors one is sometimes ashamed of. The agen-cies by which events so grand as the opening of California, of Texas, of Oregon, and the junction of the two oceans, are effected, are paltry, — coarse selfishness, fraud and conspiracy ; and most of the great results of history are brought about by dis-creditable means.

The benefaction derived in Illinois and the great West from railroads is inestimable, and vastly ex-ceeding any intentional philanthropy on record. What is the benefit done by a good King Alfred, or by a Howard, or Pestalozzi, or Elizabeth Fry, or Florence Nightingale, or any lover, less or

larger, compared with the involuntary blessing
wrought on nations by the selfish capitalists who
built the Illinois, Michigan, and the network of the
Mississippi-valley roads; which have evoked not
only all the wealth of the soil, but the energy of
millions of men. It is a sentence of ancient wisdom that " God hangs the greatest weights on the
smallest wires."

What happens thus to nations, befalls every day
in private houses. When the friends of a gentleman brought to his notice the follies of his sons,
with many hints of their danger, he replied that he
knew so much mischief when he was a boy, and
had turned out on the whole so successfully, that
he was not alarmed by the dissipation of boys;
't was dangerous water, but he thought they would
soon touch bottom, and then swim to the top. This
is bold practice, and there are many failures to a
good escape. Yet one would say that a good understanding would suffice as well as moral sensibility to keep one erect; the gratifications of the passions are so quickly seen to be damaging, and —
what men like least — seriously lowering them in
social rank. Then all talent sinks with character.

" *Croyez moi, l'erreur aussi a son mérite,*" said
Voltaire. We see those who surmount, by dint of
some egotism or infatuation, obstacles from which
the prudent recoil. The right partisan is a heady

narrow man, who, because he does not see many
things, sees some one thing with heat and exaggeration, and if he falls among other narrow men, or
on objects which have a brief importance, as some
trade or politics of the hour, he prefers it to the
universe, and seems inspired and a godsend to
those who wish to magnify the matter and carry
a point. Better, certainly, if we could secure the
strength and fire which rude, passionate men bring
into society, quite clear of their vices. But who
dares draw out the linchpin from the wagon-wheel?
'T is so manifest that there is no moral deformity
but is a good passion out of place ; that there is no
man who is not indebted to his foibles ; that, according to the old oracle, "the Furies are the bonds
of men ;" that the poisons are our principal med-
icines, which kill the disease and save the life. In
the high prophetic phrase, *He causes the wrath of
man to praise him,* and twists and wrenches our
evil to our good. Shakspeare wrote, —

"'T is said, best men are moulded of their faults ;"

and great educators and lawgivers, and especially
generals and leaders of colonies, mainly rely on this
stuff, and esteem men of irregular and passional
force the best timber. A man of sense and energy,
the late head of the Farm School in Boston Harbor, said to me, "I want none of your good boys, —

give me the bad ones." And this is the reason, I suppose, why, as soon as the children are good, the mothers are scared, and think they are going to die. Mirabeau said, " There are none but men of strong passions capable of going to greatness ; none but such capable of meriting the public gratitude." Passion, though a bad regulator, is a powerful spring. Any absorbing passion has the effect to deliver from the little coils and cares of every day : 't is the heat which sets our human atoms spinning, overcomes the friction of crossing thresholds and first addresses in society, and gives us a good start and speed, easy to continue when once it is begun. In short there is no man who is not at some time indebted to his vices, as no plant that is not fed from manures. We only insist that the man meliorate, and that the plant grow upward and convert the base into the better nature.

The wise workman will not regret the poverty or the solitude which brought out his working talents. The youth is charmed with the fine air and accomplishments of the children of fortune. But all great men come out of the middle classes. 'T is better for the head ; 't is better for the heart. Marcus Antoninus says that Fronto told him that " the so-called high-born are for the most part heartless ; " whilst nothing is so indicative of deepest culture as a tender consideration of the ignorant. Charles James Fox said of England, " The history of this country proves that we are not to expect from men in affluent circumstances the vigilance, energy, and exertion without which the House of Commons would lose its greatest force and weight. Human nature is prone to indulgence, and the most meritorious public services have always been performed by persons in a condition of life removed from opulence." And yet what we ask daily, is to be conventional. Supply, most kind gods! this defect in my address, in my form, in my fortunes, which puts me a little out of the ring: supply it, and let me be like the rest whom I admire, and on good terms with them. But the wise gods say, No, we have better things for thee. By humiliations, by defeats, by loss of sympathy, by gulfs of disparity, learn a wider truth and humanity than that of a fine gentleman. A Fifth-Avenue landlord, a West-End householder, is not the highest style of man; and though good hearts and sound minds are of no condition, yet he who is to be wise for many must not be protected. He must know the huts where poor men lie, and the chores which poor men do. The first-class minds, Æsop, Socrates, Cervantes, Shakspeare, Franklin, had the poor man's feeling and mortification. A rich man was never insulted in his life; but this man must be stung. A rich man was never in danger from cold, or hunger, or war, or ruffians, — and you can see he was not, from the moderation of his ideas. 'T is a fatal disadvantage to be cockered and to eat too much cake. What tests of manhood could he stand? Take him out of his protections. He is a good book-keeper; or he is a shrewd adviser in the insurance office; perhaps he could pass a college examination, and take his degrees; perhaps he can give wise counsel in a court of law. Now plant him down among farmers, firemen, Indians, and emigrants. Set a dog on him; set a highwayman on him; try him with a course of mobs; send him to Kansas, to Pike's Peak, to Oregon; and, if he have true faculty, this may be the element he wants, and he will come out of it with broader wisdom and manly power. Æsop, Saadi, Cervantes, Regnard, have been taken by corsairs, left for dead, sold for slaves, and know the realities of human life.

Bad times have a scientific value. These are occasions a good learner would not miss. As we go gladly to Faneuil Hall to be played upon by the stormy winds and strong fingers of enraged patriotism, so is a fanatical persecution, civil war, national bankruptcy or revolution more rich in the central tones than languid years of prosperity. What had been, ever since our memory, solid continent, yawns apart and discloses its composition and genesis. We learn geology the morning after the earthquake, on ghastly diagrams of cloven mountains, upheaved plains, and the dry bed of the sea.

In our life and culture everything is worked up and comes in use, — passion, war, revolt, bankruptcy, and not less, folly and blunders, insult, ennui and bad company. Nature is a rag-merchant, who works up every shred and ort and end into new creations; like a good chemist whom I found the other day in his laboratory, converting his old shirts into pure white sugar. Life is a boundless privilege, and when you pay for your ticket and get into the car, you have no guess what good company you shall find there. You buy much that is not rendered in the bill. Men achieve a certain greatness unawares, when working to another aim.

If now in this connection of discourse we should venture on laying down the first obvious rules of life, I will not here repeat the first rule of economy, already propounded once and again, that every man shall maintain himself, — but I will say, get health. No labor, pains, temperance, poverty, nor exercise, that can gain it, must be grudged. For sickness is a cannibal which eats up all the life and youth it can lay hold of, and absorbs its own sons and daughters. I figure it as a pale, wailing, distracted phantom, absolutely selfish, heedless of what is good and great, attentive to its sensations, losing its soul, and afflicting other souls with mean-ness and mopings and with ministration to its vorac-ity of trifles. Dr. Johnson said severely, "Every man is a rascal as soon as he is sick." Drop the cant, and treat it sanely. In dealing with the drunken, we do not affect to be drunk. We must treat the sick with the same firmness, giving them of course every aid, — but withholding ourselves. I once asked a clergyman in a retired town, who were his companions? what men of ability he saw? He replied that he spent his time with the sick and the dying. I said he seemed to me to need quite other company, and all the more that he had this ; for if people were sick and dying to any purpose, we would leave all and go to them, but as far as I had observed they were as frivolous as the rest, and sometimes much more frivolous. Let us engage our companions not to spare us. I knew a wise woman who said to her friends, "When I am old, rule me." And the best part of health is fine dis-position. It is more essential than talent, even in the works of talent. Nothing will supply the want of sunshine to peaches, and to make knowledge val-uable, you must have the cheerfulness of wisdom. Whenever you are sincerely pleased, you are nour-ished. The joy of the spirit indicates its strength. All healthy things are sweet - tempered. Genius works in sport, and goodness smiles to the last;

and for the reason that whoever sees the law which distributes things, does not despond, but is animated to great desires and endeavors. He who desponds betrays that he has not seen it.

'T is a Dutch proverb that "paint costs nothing," such are its preserving qualities in damp climates. Well, sunshine costs less, yet is finer pigment. And so of cheerfulness, or a good temper, the more it is spent, the more of it remains. The latent heat of an ounce of wood or stone is inexhaustible. You may rub the same chip of pine to the point of kindling a hundred times; and the power of happiness of any soul is not to be computed or drained. It is observed that a depression of spirits develops the germs of a plague in individuals and nations.

It is an old commendation of right behavior, " *Aliis lœtus, sapiens sibi*," which our English proverb translates, " Be merry *and* wise." I know how easy it is to men of the world to look grave and sneer at your sanguine youth and its glittering dreams. But I find the gayest castles in the air that were ever piled, far better for comfort and for use than the dungeons in the air that are daily dug and caverned out by grumbling, discontented people. I know those miserable fellows, and I hate them, who see a black star always riding through the light and colored clouds in the sky overhead:

waves of light pass over and hide it for a moment, but the black star keeps fast in the zenith. But power dwells with cheerfulness; hope puts us in a working mood, whilst despair is no muse, and untunes the active powers. A man should make life and Nature happier to us, or he had better never been born. When the political economist reckons up the unproductive classes, he should put at the head this class of pitiers of themselves, cravers of sympathy, bewailing imaginary disasters. An old French verse runs, in my translation : —

> " Some of your griefs you have cured,
>   And the sharpest you still have survived;
> But what torments of pain you endured
>   From evils that never arrived ! "

There are three wants which never can be satisfied : that of the rich, who wants something more; that of the sick, who wants something different; and that of the traveller, who says, 'Anywhere but here.' The Turkish cadi said to Layard, " After the fashion of thy people, thou hast wandered from one place to another, until thou art happy and content in none." My countrymen are not less infatuated with the *rococo* toy of Italy. All America seems on the point of embarking for Europe. But we shall not always traverse seas and lands with light purposes, and for pleasure, as we say. One day we shall cast out the passion for Europe by the passion for America. Culture will give gravity and domestic rest to those who now travel only as not knowing how else to spend money. Already, who provoke pity like that excellent family party just arriving in their well-appointed carriage, as far from home and any honest end as ever? Each nation has asked successively, ' What are they here for?' until at last the party are shamefaced, and anticipate the question at the gates of each town.

Genial manners are good, and power of accommodation to any circumstance; but the high prize of life, the crowning fortune of a man, is to be born with a bias to some pursuit which finds him in employment and happiness, — whether it be to make baskets, or broadswords, or canals, or statutes, or songs. I doubt not this was the meaning of Socrates, when he pronounced artists the only truly wise, as being actually, not apparently so.

In childhood we fancied ourselves walled in by the horizon, as by a glass bell, and doubted not by distant travel we should reach the baths of the descending sun and stars. On experiment the horizon flies before us and leaves us on an endless common, sheltered by no glass bell. Yet 't is strange how tenaciously we cling to that bell-astronomy of a protecting domestic horizon. I find the same illusion in the search after happiness which I observe every summer recommenced in this neighborhood, soon after the pairing of the birds. The young people do not like the town, do not like the sea-shore, they will go inland ; find a dear cottage deep in the mountains, secret as their hearts. They set forth on their travels in search of a home : they reach Berkshire ; they reach Vermont ; they look at the farms ; — good farms, high mountain-sides ; but where is the seclusion? The farm is near this, 't is near that ; they have got far from Boston, but 't is near Albany, or near Burlington, or near Montreal. They explore a farm, but the house is small, old, thin ; discontented people lived there and are gone ; — there's too much sky, too much out-doors ; too public. The youth aches for solitude. When he comes to the house he passes through the house. That does not make the deep recess he sought. 'Ah! now I perceive,' he says, 'it must be deep with persons; friends only can give depth.' Yes, but there is a great dearth, this year, of friends ; hard to find, and hard to have when found : they are just going away ; they too are in the whirl of the flitting world, and have engagements and necessities. They are just starting for Wisconsin ; have letters from Bremen ; — see you again, soon. Slow, slow to learn the lesson that there is but one depth, but one interior, and that is — his purpose. When joy or calamity or genius shall show him it, then woods, then farms, then city shopmen and cabdrivers, indifferently with prophet or friend, will mirror back to him its unfathomable heaven, its populous solitude.

The uses of travel are occasional, and short; but the best fruit it finds, when it finds it, is conversation; and this is a main function of life. What a difference in the hospitality of minds! Inestimable is he to whom we can say what we cannot say to ourselves. Others are involuntarily hurtful to us and bereave us of the power of thought, impound and imprison us. As, when there is sympathy, there needs but one wise man in a company and all are wise, so a blockhead makes a blockhead of his companion. Wonderful power to benumb possesses this brother. When he comes into the office or public room, the society dissolves; one after another slips out, and the apartment is at his disposal. What is incurable but a frivolous habit? A fly is as untamable as a hyena. Yet folly in the sense of fun, fooling or dawdling can easily be borne; as Talleyrand said, " I find nonsense singularly refreshing;" but a virulent, aggressive fool taints the reason of a household. I have seen a whole family of quiet, sensible people unhinged and beside themselves, victims of such a rogue. For the steady wrongheadedness of one perverse person irritates the best; since we must withstand absurdity. But resistance only exasperates the acrid fool, who believes that Nature and gravitation are quite wrong, and he only is right. Hence all the dozen inmates are soon perverted, with whatever virtues and industries they have, into contradictors, accusers, explainers and repairers of this one malefactor; like a boat about to be overset, or a carriage run away with, — not only the foolish pilot or driver, but everybody on board is forced to assume strange and ridiculous attitudes, to balance the vehicle and prevent the upsetting. For remedy, whilst the case is yet mild, I recommend phlegm and truth: let all the truth that is spoken or done be at the zero of indifferency, or truth itself will be folly. But when the case is seated and malignant, the only safety is in amputation; as seamen say, you shall cut and run. How to live with unfit companions? — for with such, life is for the most part spent; and experience teaches little better than our earliest instinct of self-defence, namely not to engage, not to mix yourself in any manner with them, but let their madness spend itself unopposed.

Conversation is an art in which a man has all mankind for his competitors, for it is that which all are practising every day while they live. Our habit of thought — take men as they rise, — is not satisfying; in the common experience I fear it is poor and squalid. The success which will content them is a bargain, a lucrative employment, an ad-

vantage gained over a competitor, a marriage, a
patrimony, a legacy, and the like. With these objects, their conversation deals with surfaces : politics, trade, personal defects, exaggerated bad news,
and the rain. This is forlorn, and they feel sore
and sensitive. Now if one comes who can illumi-
nate this dark house with thoughts, show them
their native riches, what gifts they have, how indis-
pensable each is, what magical powers over nature
and men ; what access to poetry, religion, and the
powers which constitute character, — he wakes in
them the feeling of worth, his suggestions require
new ways of living, new books, new men, new arts
and sciences ; —then we come out of our egg-shell
existence into the great dome, and see the zenith
over and the nadir under us. Instead of the
tanks and buckets of knowledge to which we are
daily confined, we come down to the shore of the
sea, and dip our hands in its miraculous waves.
'T is wonderful the effect on the company. They
are not the men they were. They have all been to
California and all have come back millionaires.
There is no book and no pleasure in life comparable
to it. Ask what is best in our experience, and we
shall say, a few pieces of plain-dealing with wise
people. Our conversation once and again has ap-
prised us that we belong to better circles than we
have yet beheld ; that a mental power invites us

whose generalizations are more worth for joy and for effect than anything that is now called philosophy or literature. In excited conversation we have glimpses of the Universe, hints of power native to the soul, far-darting lights and shadows of an Andes landscape, such as we can hardly attain in lone meditation. Here are oracles sometimes profusely given, to which the memory goes back in barren hours.

Add the consent of will and temperament, and there exists the covenant of friendship. Our chief want in life is somebody who shall make us do what we can. This is the service of a friend. With him we are easily great. There is a sublime attraction in him to whatever virtue is in us. How he flings wide the doors of existence! What questions we ask of him! what an understanding we have! how few words are needed! It is the only real society. An Eastern poet, Ali Ben Abu Taleb, writes with sad truth : —

" He who has a thousand friends has not a friend to spare,
    And he who has one enemy shall meet him everywhere."

But few writers have said anything better to this point than Hafiz, who indicates this relation as the test of mental health : " Thou learnest no secret until thou knowest friendship, since to the unsound no heavenly knowledge enters." Neither is life long enough for friendship. That is a serious and majestic affair, like a royal presence, or a religion, and not a postilion's dinner to be eaten on the run. There is a pudency about friendship as about love, and though fine souls never lose sight of it, yet they do not name it. With the first class of men our friendship or good understanding goes quite behind all accidents of estrangement, of condition, of reputation. And yet we do not provide for the greatest good of life. We take care of our health; we lay up money; we make our roof tight, and our clothing sufficient; but who provides wisely that he shall not be wanting in the best property of all, — friends? We know that all our training is to fit us for this, and we do not take the step towards it. How long shall we sit and wait for these benefactors?

It makes no difference, in looking back five years, how you have been dieted or dressed; whether you have been lodged on the first floor or the attic; whether you have had gardens and baths, good cattle and horses, have been carried in a neat equipage, or in a ridiculous truck: these things are forgotten so quickly, and leave no effect. But it counts much whether we have had good companions in that time, — almost as much as what we have been doing. And see the overpowering importance of neighborhood in all association. As it is marriage, fit or unfit, that makes our home,

so it is who lives near us of equal social degree, —
a few people at convenient distance, no matter how
bad company, — these, and these only, shall be
your life's companions; and all those who are native, congenial, and by many an oath of the heart
sacramented to you, are gradually and totally lost.
You cannot deal systematically with this fine element of society, and one may take a good deal
of pains to bring people together and to organize clubs and debating societies, and yet no result
come of it.   But it is certain that there is a great
deal of good in us that does not know itself, and
that a habit of union and competition brings people up and keeps them up to their highest point;
that life would be twice or ten times life if spent
with wise and fruitful companions. The obvious
inference is, a little useful deliberation and pre-
concert when one goes to buy house and land.

   But we live with people on other platforms;
we live with dependents; not only with the young
whom we are to teach all we know and clothe with
the advantages we have earned, but also with those
who serve us directly, and for money. Yet the old
rules hold good. Let not the tie be mercenary,
though the service is measured by money. Make
yourself necessary to somebody. Do not make life
hard to any. This point is acquiring new importance in American social life. Our domestic ser-

vice is usually a foolish fracas of unreasonable demand on one side and shirking on the other. A
man of wit was asked, in the train, what was his
errand in the city? He replied, "I have been sent
to procure an angel to do cooking." A lady complained to me that of her two maidens, one was
absent-minded and the other was absent-bodied.
And the evil increases from the ignorance and hos-
tility of every ship-load of the immigrant population
swarming into houses and farms. Few people discern that it rests with the master or the mistress
what service comes from the man or the maid;
that this identical hussy was a tutelar spirit in one
house and a haridan in the other. All sensible
people are selfish, and nature is tugging at every
contract to make the terms of it fair. If you are
proposing only your own, the other party must deal
a little hardly by you. If you deal generously, the
other, though selfish and unjust, will make an exception in your favor, and deal truly with you.
When I asked an iron-master about the slag and
cinder in railroad iron, — " O," he said, " there's
always good iron to be had: if there's cinder
in the iron it is because there was cinder in the
pay."

But why multiply these topics, and their illus-
trations, which are endless? Life brings to each
his task, and whatever art you select, algebra,

planting, architecture,. poems, commerce, politics, —
all are attainable, even to the miraculous triumphs,
on the same terms of selecting that for which you
are apt; begin at the beginning, proceed in order,
step by step. 'T is as easy to twist iron anchors
and braid cannons as to braid straw; to boil granite
as to boil water, if you take all the steps in order.
Wherever there is failure, there is some giddiness,
some superstition about luck, some step omitted,
which Nature never pardons. The happy conditions of life may be had on the same terms. Their
attraction for you is the pledge that they are within
your reach. Our prayers are prophets. There
must be fidelity, and there must be adherence.
How respectable the life that clings to its objects!
Youthful aspirations are fine things, your theories
and plans of life are fair and commendable : —
but will you stick? Not one, I fear, in that Common full of people, or, in a thousand, but one: and
when you tax them with treachery, and remind
them of their high resolutions, they have forgotten
that they made a vow. The individuals are fugitive, and in the act of becoming something else,
and irresponsible. The race is great, the ideal fair,
but the men whiffling and unsure. The hero is he
who is immovably centred. The main difference
between people seems to be that one man can
come under obligations on which you can rely, — is

obligable; and another is not. As he has not a
law within him, there's nothing to tie him to.

It is inevitable to name particulars of virtue and
of condition, and to exaggerate them. But all rests
at last on that integrity which dwarfs talent, and
can spare it. Sanity consists in not being subdued
by your means. Fancy prices are paid for position
and for the culture of talent, but to the grand
interests, superficial success is of no account. The
man, — it is his attitude, — not feats, but forces, —
not on set days and public occasions, but at all
hours, and in repose alike as in energy, still formidable and not to be disposed of. The populace
says, with Horne Tooke, "If you would be powerful, pretend to be powerful." I prefer to say,
with the old prophet, "Seekest thou great things?
seek them not:" — or, what was said of a Spanish
prince, "The more you took from him, the greater
he looked." *Plus on lui ôte, plus il est grand.*

The secret of culture is to learn that a few great
points steadily reappear, alike in the poverty of the
obscurest farm and in the miscellany of metropol-
itan life, and that these few are alone to be re-
garded; — the escape from all false ties; courage
to be what we are, and love of what is simple
and beautiful; independence and cheerful relation,
these are the essentials, — these, and the wish to
serve, to add somewhat to the well-being of men.

VIII.

BEAUTY.

—◆—

Was never form and never face
So sweet to Seyd as only grace
Which did not slumber like a stone
But hovered gleaming and was gone.
Beauty chased he everywhere,
In flame, in storm, in clouds of air.
He smote the lake to feed his eye
   With the beryl beam of the broken wave.
He flung in pebbles well to hear
   The moment's music which they gave.
Oft pealed for him a lofty tone
From nodding pole and belting zone.
He heard a voice none else could hear
From centred and from errant sphere.
The quaking earth did quake in rhyme,
Seas ebbed and flowed in epic chime.
In dens of passion, and pits of woe,
He saw strong Eros struggling through,
To sun the dark and solve the curse,
And beam to the bounds of the universe.
While thus to love he gave his days

In loyal worship, scorning praise,
How spread their lures for him, in vain,
Thieving ambition and paltering Gain!
He thought it happier to be dead,
To die for Beauty, than live for bread.

BEAUTY.

THE spiral tendency of vegetation infects education also. Our books approach very slowly the things we most wish to know. What a parade we make of our science, and how far off and at arm's length it is from its objects! Our botany is all names, not powers: poets and romancers talk of herbs of grace and healing, but what does the botanist know of the virtues of his weeds? The geologist lays bare the strata and can tell them all on his fingers; but does he know what effect passes into the man who builds his house in them? what effect on the race that inhabits a granite shelf? what on the inhabitants of marl and of alluvium?

. We should go to the ornithologist with a new feeling if he could teach us what the social birds say when they sit in the autumn council, talking together in the trees. The want of sympathy makes his record a dull dictionary. His result is a dead bird. The bird is not in its ounces and inches, but in its relations to Nature; and the skin or skeleton you show me is no more a heron, than a heap of ashes or a bottle of gases into which his body has been reduced, is Dante or Washington. The naturalist is led *from* the road by the whole distance of his fancied advance. The boy had juster views when he gazed at the shells on the beach or the flowers in the meadow, unable to call them by their names, than the man in the pride of his nomenclature. Astrology interested us, for it tied man to the system. Instead of an isolated beggar, the farthest star felt him and he felt the star. However rash and however falsified by pretenders and traders in it, the hint was true and divine, the soul's avowal of its large relations, and that climate, century, remote natures as well as near, are part of its biography. Chemistry takes to pieces, but it does not construct. Alchemy, which sought to transmute one element into another, to prolong life, to arm with power, — that was in the right direction. All our science lacks a human side. The tenant is more than the house. Bugs and stamens and spores, on which we lavish so many years, are not finalities; and man, when his powers unfold in order, will take Nature along with him, and emit light into all her recesses. The human heart concerns us more than the poring into microscopes, and is larger than can be measured by the pompous figures of the astronomer.

We are just so frivolous and skeptical. Men hold themselves cheap and vile; and yet a man is a fagot of thunderbolts. All the elements pour through his system; he is the flood of the flood and fire of the fire; he feels the antipodes and the pole as drops of his blood; they are the extension of his personality. His duties are measured by that instrument he is; and a right and perfect man would be felt to the centre of the Copernican system. 'T is curious that we only believe as deep as we live. We do not think heroes can exert any more awful power than that surface - play which amuses us. A deep man believes in miracles, waits for them, believes in magic, believes that the orator will decompose his adversary; .believes that the evil eye can wither, that the heart's blessing can heal; that love can exalt talent; can overcome all odds. From a great heart secret magnetisms flow incessantly to draw great events. But we prize very humble utilities, a prudent husband, a good son, a voter, a citizen, and deprecate any romance of character; and perhaps reckon only his money value, his intellect, his affection, — as a sort of bill of exchange easily convertible into fine chambers, pictures, music, and wine.

The motive of science was the extension of man, on all sides, into Nature, till his hands should touch the stars, his eyes see through the earth, his ears understand the language of beast and bird, and the sense of the wind; and, through his sympathy,

heaven and earth should talk with him. But that
is not our science. These geologies, chemistries,
astronomies, seem to make wise, but they leave us
where they found us. The invention is of use to
the inventor, of questionable help to any other.
The formulas of science are like the papers in your
pocket - book, of no value to any but the owner.
Science in England, in America, is jealous of theory, hates the name of love and moral purpose.
There's a revenge for this inhumanity. What
manner of man does science make? The boy is
not attracted. He says, I do not wish to be such
a kind of man as my professor is. The collector
has dried all the plants in his herbal, but he has
lost weight and humor. He has got all snakes and
lizards in his phials, but science has done for him
also, and has put the man into a bottle. Our reliance on the physician is a kind of despair of ourselves. The clergy have bronchitis, which does not
seem a certificate of spiritual health. Macready
thought it came of the *falsetto* of their voicing.
An Indian prince, Tisso, one day riding in the forest, saw a herd of elk sporting. "See how happy,"
he said, "these browsing elks are! Why should
not priests, lodged and fed comfortably in the temples, also amuse themselves?" Returning home,
he imparted this reflection to the king. The king,
on the next day, conferred the sovereignty on him,

saying, " Prince, administer this empire for seven
days ; at the termination of that period I shall put
thee to death." At the end of the seventh day
the king inquired, "From what cause hast thou become so emaciated ? " He answered, "From the
horror of death." The monarch rejoined, "Live,
my child, and be wise. Thou hast ceased to take
recreation, saying to thyself, In seven days I shall
be put to death. These priests in the temple incessantly meditate on death ; how can they enter into
healthful diversions ? " But the men of science or
the doctors or the clergy are not victims of their
pursuits more than others. The miller, the lawyer,
and the merchant, dedicate themselves to their own
details, and do not come out men of more force.
Have they divination, grand aims, hospitality of
soul, and the equality to any event which we demand in man, or only the reactions of the mill, of
the wares, of the chicane ?

No object really interests us but man, and in
man only his superiorities ; and though we are
aware of a perfect law in Nature, it has fascination
for us only through its relation to him, or as it
is rooted in the mind. At the birth of Winckelmann, more than a hundred years ago, side by side
with this arid, departmental, *post mortem* science,
rose an enthusiasm in the study of Beauty; and
perhaps some sparks from it may yet light a con-

flagration in the other. Knowledge of men, knowledge of manners, the power of form, and our sensibility to personal influence never go out of fashion. These are facts of a science which we study without book, whose teachers and subjects are always near us.

So inveterate is our habit of criticism that much of our knowledge in this direction belongs to the chapter of pathology. The crowd in the street oftener furnishes degradations than angels or redeemers, but they all prove the transparency. Every spirit makes its house, and we can give a shrewd guess from the house to the inhabitant. But not less does Nature furnish us with every sign of grace and goodness. The delicious faces of children, the beauty of school-girls, " the sweet seriousness of sixteen," the lofty air of well-born, well-bred boys, the passionate histories in the looks and manners of youth and early manhood, and the varied power in all that well-known company that escort us through life, — we know how these forms thrill, paralyze, provoke, inspire, and enlarge us.

Beauty is the form under which the intellect prefers to study the world. All privilege is that of beauty; for there are many beauties; as, of general nature, of the human face and form, of manners, of brain or method, moral beauty or beauty of the soul.

The ancients believed that a genius or demon took possession at birth of each mortal, to guide him ; that these genii were sometimes seen as a flame of fire partly immersed in the bodies which they governed; on an evil man, resting on his head; in a good man, mixed with his substance. They thought the same genius, at the death of its ward, entered a new-born child, and they pretended to guess the pilot by the sailing of the ship. We recognize obscurely the same fact, though we give it our own names. We say that every man is entitled to be valued by his best moment. We measure our friends so. We know they have intervals of folly, whereof we take no heed, but wait the reappearings of the genius, which are sure and beautiful. On the other side, everybody knows people who appear beridden, and who, with all degrees of ability, never impress us with the air of free agency. They know it too, and peep with their eyes to see if you detect their sad plight. We fancy, could we pronounce the solving word and disenchant them, the cloud would roll up, the little rider would be discovered and unseated, and they would regain their freedom. The remedy seems never to be far off, since the first step into thought lifts this mountain of necessity. Thought is the pent air-ball which can rive the planet, and the beauty which certain objects have for him is the

friendly fire which expands the thought and ac-
quaints the prisoner that liberty and power await
him.

The question of Beauty takes us out of surfaces
to thinking of the foundations of things. Goethe
said, "The beautiful is a manifestation of secret
laws of Nature which, but for this appearance, had
been forever concealed from us." And the working of this deep instinct makes all the excitement
— much of it superficial and absurd enough —
about works of art, which leads armies of vain
travellers every year to Italy, Greece, and Egypt.
Every man values every acquisition he makes in
the science of beauty, above his possessions. The
most useful man in the most useful world, so long
as only commodity was served, would remain un-
satisfied. But as fast as he sees beauty, life acquires a very high value.

I am warned by the ill fate of many philosophers
not to attempt a definition of Beauty. I will rather
enumerate a few of its qualities. We ascribe beauty
to that which is simple; which has no superfluous
parts; which exactly answers its end; which stands
related to all things; which is the mean of many
extremes. It is the most enduring quality, and the
most ascending quality. We say love is blind, and
the figure of Cupid is drawn with a bandage round
his eyes. Blind: yes, because he does not see what

he does not like ; but the sharpest-sighted hunter
in the universe is Love, for finding what he seeks,
and only that; and the mythologists tell us that
Vulcan was painted lame and Cupid blind, to call
attention to the fact that one was all limbs, and
the other all eyes. In the true mythology Love
is an immortal child, and Beauty leads him as a
guide: nor can we express a deeper sense than
when we say, Beauty is the pilot of the young soul.

Beyond their sensuous delight, the forms and
colors of Nature have a new charm for us in our
perception that not one ornament was added for
ornament, but each is a sign of some better health
or more excellent action. Elegance of form in bird
or beast, or in the human figure, marks some excellence of structure : or, beauty is only an invitation from what belongs to us. 'Tis a law of botany that in plants the same virtues follow the same
forms. It is a rule of largest application, true in
a plant, true in a loaf of bread, that in the con-
struction of any fabric or organism any real increase of fitness to its end is an increase of beauty.

The lesson taught by the study of Greek and of
Gothic art, of antique and of Pre-Raphaelite painting, was worth all the research, — namely, that all
beauty must be organic ; that outside embellish-
ment is deformity. It is the soundness of the
bones that ultimates itself in a peach-bloom com-

plexion ; health of constitution that makes the sparkle and the power of the eye. 'T is the adjustment of the size and of the joining of the sockets of the skeleton that gives grace of outline and the finer grace of movement. The cat and the deer cannot move or sit inelegantly. The dancingmaster can never teach a badly built man to walk well. The tint of the flower proceeds from its root, and the lustres of the sea-shell begin with its existence. Hence our taste in building rejects paint, and all shifts, and shows the original grain of the wood : refuses pilasters and columns that support nothing, and allows the real supporters of the house honestly to show themselves. Every necessary or organic action pleases the beholder. A man leading a horse to water, a farmer sowing seed, the labors of haymakers in the field, the carpenter building a ship, the smith at his forge, or whatever useful labor, is becoming to the wise eye. But if it is done to be seen, it is mean. How beautiful are ships on the sea ! but ships in the theatre, — or ships kept for picturesque effect on Virginia Water by George IV., and men hired to stand in fitting costumes at a penny an hour ! What a difference in effect between a battalion of troops marching to action, and one of our independent companies on a holiday ! In the midst of a military show and a festal procession gay with

banners, I saw a boy seize an old tin pan that lay
rusting under a wall, and poising it on the top of a
stick, he set it turning and made it describe the
most elegant imaginable curves, and drew away
attention from the decorated procession by this
startling beauty.

Another text from the mythologists. The
Greeks fabled that Venus was born of the foam of
the sea. Nothing interests us which is stark or
bounded, but only what streams with life, what is
in act or endeavor to reach somewhat beyond. The
pleasure a palace or a temple gives the eye is, that
an order and method has been communicated to
stones, so that they speak and geometrize, become
tender or sublime with expression. Beauty is the
moment of transition, as if the form were just
ready to flow into other forms. Any fixedness,
heaping, or concentration on one feature, — a long
nose, a sharp chin, a hump-back, — is the reverse
of the flowing, and therefore deformed. Beautiful
as is the symmetry of any form, if the form can
move we seek a more excellent symmetry. The
interruption of equilibrium stimulates the eye to
desire the restoration of symmetry, and to watch
the steps through which it is attained. This is the
charm of running water, sea-waves, the flight of
birds and the locomotion of animals. This is the
theory of dancing, to recover continually in changes

the lost equilibrium, not by abrupt and angular but by gradual and curving movements. I have been told by persons of experience in matters of taste that the fashions follow a law of gradation, and are never arbitrary. The new mode is always only a step onward in the same direction as the last mode, and a cultivated eye is prepared for and predicts the new fashion. This fact suggests the reason of all mistakes and offence in our own modes. It is necessary in music, when you strike a discord, to let down the ear by an intermediate note or two to the accord again; and many a good experiment, born of good sense and destined to suc ceed, fails only because it is offensively sudden. I suppose the Parisian milliner who dresses the world from her imperious boudoir will know how to rec-oncile the Bloomer costume to the eye of mankind, and make it triumphant over Punch himself, by interposing the just gradations. I need not say how wide the same law ranges, and how much it can be hoped to effect. All that is a little harshly claimed by progressive parties may easily come to be conceded without question, if this rule be ob-served. Thus the circumstances may be easily im-agined in which woman may speak, vote, argue causes, legislate, and drive a coach, and all the most naturally in the world, if only it come by degrees. To this streaming or flowing belongs the beauty that

all circular movement has; as the circulation of
waters, the circulation of the blood, the periodical
motion of planets, the annual wave of vegetation,
the action and reaction of Nature; and if we follow
it out, this demand in our thought for an ever-
onward action is the argument for the immortality.

One more text from the mythologists is to the
same purpose, — *Beauty rides on a lion.* Beauty
rests on necessities. The line of beauty is the result of perfect economy. The cell of the bee is
built at that angle which gives the most strength
with the least wax; the bone or the quill of the
bird gives the most alar strength with the least
weight. "It is the purgation of superfluities," said
Michael Angelo. There is not a particle to spare
in natural structures. There is a compelling reason in the uses of the plant for every novelty of
color or form; and our art saves material by more
skilful arrangement, and reaches beauty by taking
every superfluous ounce that can be spared from a
wall, and keeping all its strength in the poetry of
columns. In rhetoric, this art of omission is a
chief secret of power, and, in general, it is proof
of high culture to say the greatest matters in the
simplest way.

Veracity first of all, and forever. *Rien de beau
que le vrai.* In all design, art lies in making your

object prominent, but there is a prior art in choosing objects that are prominent. The fine arts have nothing casual, but spring from the instincts of the nations that created them.

Beauty is the quality which makes to endure. In a house that I know, I have noticed a block of spermaceti lying about closets and mantel-pieces, for twenty years together, simply because the tallow-man gave it the form of a rabbit; and I suppose it may continue to be lugged about unchanged for a century. Let an artist scrawl a few lines or figures on the back of a letter, and that scrap of paper is rescued from danger, is put in portfolio, is framed and glazed, and, in proportion to the beauty of the lines drawn, will be kept for centuries. Burns writes a copy of verses and sends them to a newspaper, and the human race take charge of them that they shall not perish.

As the flute is heard farther than the cart, see how surely a beautiful form strikes the fancy of men, and is copied and reproduced without end. How many copies are there of the Belvedere Apollo, the Venus, the Psyche, the Warwick Vase, the Parthenon and the Temple of Vesta? These are objects of tenderness to all. In our cities an ugly building is soon removed and is never repeated, but any beautiful building is copied and improved upon, so that all masons and carpenters work to repeat and preserve the agreeable forms, whilst the ugly ones die out.

The felicities of design in art or in works of Nature are shadows or forerunners of that beauty which reaches its perfection in the human form. All men are its lovers. Wherever it goes it creates joy and hilarity, and everything is permitted to it. It reaches its height in woman. " To Eve," say the Mahometans, " God gave two thirds of all beauty." A beautiful woman is a practical poet, taming her savage mate, planting tenderness, hope, and eloquence in all whom she approaches. Some favors of condition must go with it, since a certain serenity is essential, but we love its reproofs and superiorities. Nature wishes that woman should attract man, yet she often cunningly moulds into her face a little sarcasm, which seems to say, ' Yes, I am willing to attract, but to attract a little better kind of man than any I yet behold.' French *mémoires* of the sixteenth century celebrate the name of Pauline de Viguier, a virtuous and accomplished maiden who so fired the enthusiasm of her contemporaries by her enchanting form, that the citizens of her native city of Toulouse obtained the aid of the civil authorities to compel her to appear publicly on the balcony at least twice a week, and as often as she showed herself, the crowd was dangerous to life. Not less in England in the last

century was the fame of the Gunnings, of whom
Elizabeth married the Duke of Hamilton, and Ma-
ria, the Earl of Coventry.   Walpole says, "The
concourse was so great, when the Duchess of Hamilton was presented at court, on Friday, that even
the noble crowd in the drawing-room clambered on
chairs and tables to look at her.   There are mobs
at their doors to see them get into their chairs, and
people go early to get places at the theatres, when
it is known they will be there."   "Such crowds,"
he adds elsewhere, "flock to see the Duchess of
Hamilton, that seven hundred people sat up all
night, in and about an inn in Yorkshire, to see her
get into her post-chaise next morning."

But why need we console ourselves with the
fames of Helen of Argos, or Corinna, or Pauline of
Toulouse, or the Duchess of Hamilton?   We all
know this magic very well, or can divine it.   It
does not hurt weak eyes to look into beautiful eyes
never so long.   Women stand related to beautiful
Nature around us, and the enamored youth mixes
their form with moon and stars, with woods and
waters, and the pomp of summer.   They heal us of
awkwardness by their words and looks.   We observe their intellectual influence on the most serious
student.   They refine and clear his mind; teach
him to put a pleasing method into what is dry and
difficult.   We talk to them and wish to be listened

to ; we fear to fatigue them, and acquire a facility of expression which passes from conversation into habit of style.

That Beauty is the normal state is shown by the perpetual effort of Nature to attain it. Mirabeau had an ugly face on a handsome ground; and we see faces every day which have a good type but have been marred in the casting; a proof that we are all entitled to beauty, should have been beautiful if our ancestors had kept the laws, — as every lily and every rose is well. But our bodies do not fit us, but caricature and satirize us. Thus, short legs which constrain us to short mincing steps are a kind of personal insult and contumely to the owner; and long stilts again put him at perpetual disadvantage, and force him to stoop to the general level of mankind. Martial ridicules a gentleman of his day whose countenance resembled the face of a swimmer seen under water. Saadi describes a schoolmaster " so ugly and crabbed that a sight of him would derange the ecstasies of the orthodox." Faces are rarely true to any ideal type, but are a record in sculpture of a thousand anecdotes of whim and folly. Portrait-painters say that most faces and forms are irregular and unsymmetrical; have one eye blue and one gray; the nose not straight, and one shoulder higher than another; the hair unequally distributed, etc. The man is phys-

ically as well as metaphysically a thing of shreds
and patches, borrowed unequally from good and
bad ancestors, and a misfit from the start.

A beautiful person among the Greeks was
thought to betray by this sign some secret favor
of the immortal gods; and we can pardon pride,
when a woman possesses such a figure that wherever she stands or moves or leaves a shadow on
the wall, or sits for a portrait to the artist, she
confers a favor on the world. And yet — it is
not beauty that inspires the deepest passion.
Beauty without grace is the hook without the bait.
Beauty, without expression, tires. Abbé Ménage
said of the President Le Bailleul that "he was fit
for nothing but to sit for his portrait." A Greek
epigram intimates that the force of love is not
shown by the courting of beauty, but when the
like desire is inflamed for one who is ill-favored.
And petulant old gentlemen, who have chanced to
suffer some intolerable weariness from pretty people, or who have seen cut flowers to some profusion,
or who see, after a world of pains have been successfully taken for the costume, how the least mistake in sentiment takes all the beauty out of your
clothes, — affirm that the secret of ugliness consists not in irregularity, but in being uninterest-
ing.

We love any forms, however ugly, from which

great qualities shine. If command, eloquence, art
or invention exist in the most deformed person,
all the accidents that usually displease, please, and
raise esteem and wonder higher. The great orator
was an emaciated, insignificant person, but he was
all brain. Cardinal De Retz says of De Bouillon,
" With the physiognomy of an ox, he had the per-
spicacity of an eagle." It was said of Hooke, the
friend of Newton, " He is the most, and promises
the least, of any man in England." " Since I am
so ugly," said Du Guesclin, " it behooves that I be
bold." Sir Philip Sidney, the darling of mankind,
Ben Jonson tells us, " was no pleasant man in
countenance, his face being spoiled with pimples,
and of high blood, and long." Those who have
ruled human destinies like planets for thousands
of years, were not handsome men. If a man can
raise a small city to be a great kingdom, can make
bread cheap, can irrigate deserts, can join oceans by
canals, can subdue steam, can organize victory, can
lead the opinions of mankind, can enlarge knowledge, — 't is no matter whether his nose is parallel
to his spine, as it ought to be, or whether he has
a nose at all; whether his legs are straight, or
whether his legs are amputated : his deformities
will come to be reckoned ornamental and advan-
tageous on the whole. This is the triumph of
expression, degrading beauty, charming us with a

power so fine and friendly and intoxicating that it
makes admired persons insipid, and the thought of
passing our lives with them insupportable.   There
are faces so fluid with expression, so flushed and
rippled by the play of thought that we can hardly
find what the mere features really are.   When the
delicious beauty of lineaments loses its power, it is
because a more delicious beauty has appeared ; that
an interior and durable form has been disclosed.
Still, Beauty rides on her lion, as before.   Still, " it
was for beauty that the world was made."   The
lives of the Italian artists, who established a despotism of genius amidst the dukes and kings and mobs
of their stormy epoch, prove how loyal men in all
times are to a finer brain, a finer method than their
own.   If a man can cut such a head on his stone
gate-post as shall draw and keep a crowd about it
all day, by its beauty, good nature, and inscrutable
meaning ; — if a man can build a plain cottage
with such symmetry as to make all the fine palaces look cheap and vulgar ; can take such advantages of Nature that all her powers serve him ;
making use of geometry, instead of expense ; tap-
ping a mountain for his water-jet ; causing the sun
and moon to seem only the decorations of his estate ; — this is still the legitimate dominion of
beauty.

The radiance of the human form, though sometimes astonishing, is only a burst of beauty for a few years or a few months at the perfection of youth, and in most, rapidly declines. But we remain lovers of it, only transferring our interest to interior excellence. And it is not only admirable in singular and salient talents, but also in the world of manners.

But the sovereign attribute remains to be noted. Things are pretty, graceful, rich, elegant, handsome, but, until they speak to the imagination, not yet beautiful. This is the reason why beauty is still escaping out of all analysis. It is not yet possessed, it cannot be handled. Proclus says, "It swims on the light of forms." It is properly not in the form, but in the mind. It instantly deserts possession, and flies to an object in the horizon. If I could put my hand on the North Star, would it be as beautiful? The sea is lovely, but when we bathe in it the beauty forsakes all the near water. For the imagination and senses cannot be gratified at the same time. Wordsworth rightly speaks of " a light that never was on sea or land," meaning that it was supplied by the observer; and the Welsh bard warns his countrywomen, that

— " Half of their charms with Cadwallon shall die."

The new virtue which constitutes a thing beautiful is a certain cosmical quality, or a power to suggest relation to the whole world, and so lift the object out of a pitiful individuality. Every natural feature, — sea, sky, rainbow, flowers, musical tone — has in it somewhat which is not private but universal, speaks of that central benefit which is the soul of Nature, and thereby is beautiful. And in chosen men and women I find somewhat in form, speech, and manners, which is not of their person and family, but of a humane, catholic, and spiritual character, and we love them as the sky. They have a largeness of suggestion, and their face and manners carry a certain grandeur, like time and justice.

The feat of the imagination is in showing the convertibility of every thing into every other thing. Facts which had never before left their stark common sense, suddenly figure as Eleusinian mysteries. My boots and chair and candlestick are fairies in disguise, meteors and constellations. All the facts in Nature are nouns of the intellect, and make the grammar of the eternal language. Every word has a double, treble, or centuple use and meaning. What! has my stove and pepper-pot a false bottom? I cry you mercy, good shoe-box! I did not know you were a jewel-case. Chaff and dust begin to sparkle, and are clothed about with immortality. And there is a joy in perceiving the representative or symbolic character of a fact, which no bare fact

or event can ever give. There are no days in
life so memorable as those which vibrated to some
stroke of the imagination.

The poets are quite right in decking their mis-
tresses with the spoils of the landscape, flower-
gardens, gems, rainbows, flushes of morning and
stars of night, since all beauty points at identity;
and whatsoever thing does not express to me the
sea and sky, day and night, is somewhat forbidden
and wrong. Into every beautiful object there enters somewhat immeasurable and divine, and just
as much into form bounded by outlines, like mountains on the horizon, as into tones of music or
depths of space. Polarized light showed the secret
architecture of bodies; and when the *second-sight*
of the mind is opened, now one color or form or
gesture and now another has a pungency, as if a
more interior ray had been emitted, disclosing its
deep holdings in the frame of things.

The laws of this translation we do not know, or
why one feature or gesture enchants, why one word
or syllable intoxicates; but the fact is familiar that
the fine touch of the eye, or a grace of manners, or
a phrase of poetry, plants wings at our shoulders;
as if the Divinity, in his approaches, lifts away
mountains of obstruction, and deigns to draw a
truer line, which the mind knows and owns. This
is that haughty force of beauty, " *vis superba*

formæ," which the poets praise, — under calm and precise outline the immeasurable and divine; Beauty hiding all wisdom and power in its calm sky.

All high beauty has a moral element in it, and I find the antique sculpture as ethical as Marcus Antoninus; and the beauty ever in proportion to the depth of thought. Gross and obscure natures, however decorated, seem impure shambles; but character gives splendor to youth and awe to wrinkled skin and gray hairs. An adorer of truth we cannot choose but obey, and the woman who has shared with us the moral sentiment, — her locks must appear to us sublime. Thus there is a climbing scale of culture, from the first agreeable sensation which a sparkling gem or a scarlet stain affords the eye, up through fair outlines and details of the landscape, features of the human face and form, signs and tokens of thought and character in manners, up to the ineffable mysteries of the intellect. Wherever we begin, thither our steps tend: an ascent from the joy of a horse in his trappings, up to the perception of Newton that the globe on which we ride is only a larger apple falling from a larger tree; up to the perception of Plato that globe and universe are rude and early expressions of an all-dissolving Unity, — the first stair on the scale to the temple of the Mind.

IX.

ILLUSIONS.

FLOW, flow the waves hated,
Accursed, adored,
The waves of mutation:
No anchorage is.
Sleep is not, death is not;
Who seem to die live.
House you were born in,
Friends of your spring-time,
Old man and young maid,
Day's toil and its guerdon,
They are all vanishing,
Fleeing to fables,
Cannot be moored.
See the stars through them,
Through treacherous marbles.
Know, the stars yonder,
The stars everlasting,
Are fugitive also,
And emulate, vaulted,
The lambent heat-lightning,
And fire-fly's flight.

When thou dost return
On the wave's circulation,
Beholding the shimmer,
The wild dissipation,
And, out of endeavor
To change and to flow
The gas become solid,
And phantoms and nothings
Return to be things,
And endless imbroglio
Is law and the world,—
Then first shalt thou know,
That in the wild turmoil,
Horsed on the Proteus,
Thou ridest to power,
And to endurance.

ILLUSIONS.

SOME years ago, in company with an agreeable party, I spent a long summer day in exploring the Mammoth Cave in Kentucky. We traversed, through spacious galleries affording a solid masonry foundation for the town and county overhead, the six or eight black miles from the mouth of the cavern to the innermost recess which tourists visit, — a niche or grotto made of one seamless stalactite, and called, I believe, Serena's Bower. I lost the light of one day. I saw high domes and bottomless pits; heard the voice of unseen waterfalls; paddled three quarters of a mile in the deep Echo River, whose waters are peopled with the blind fish; crossed the streams "Lethe" and "Styx;" plied with music and guns the echoes in these alarming galleries; saw every form of stalagmite and stalactite in the sculptured and fretted chambers; — icicle, orange-flower, acanthus, grapes, and snowball. We shot Bengal lights into the vaults and groins of the sparry cathedrals and examined all the masterpieces which the four combined engineers, water, limestone, gravitation and time could make in the dark.

The mysteries and scenery of the cave had the same dignity that belongs to all natural objects, and which shames the fine things to which we foppishly compare them. I remarked especially the mimetic habit with which Nature, on new instruments, hums her old tunes, making night to mimic day, and chemistry to ape vegetation. But I then took notice and still chiefly remember that the best thing which the cave had to offer was an illusion. On arriving at what is called the "Star-Chamber," our lamps were taken from us by the guide and extinguished or put aside, and, on looking upwards, I saw or seemed to see the night heaven thick with stars glimmering more or less brightly over our heads, and even what seemed a comet flaming among them. All the party were touched with astonishment and pleasure. Our musical friends sung with much feeling a pretty song, "The stars are in the quiet sky," &c., and I sat down on the rocky floor to enjoy the serene picture. Some crystal specks in the black ceiling high overhead, reflecting the light of a half-hid lamp, yielded this magnificent effect.

I own I did not like the cave so well for eking out its sublimities with this theatrical trick. But I have had many experiences like it, before and since; and we must be content to be pleased without too curiously analyzing the occasions. Our conversation with Nature is not just what it seems. The cloud-rack, the sunrise and sunset glories, rainbows and Northern Lights are not quite so spheral as our childhood thought them, and the part our organization plays in them is too large. The senses interfere everywhere and mix their own structure with all they report of. Once we fancied the earth a plane, and stationary. In admiring the sunset we do not yet deduct the rounding, co-ordinating, pictorial powers of the eye.

The same interference from our organization creates the most of our pleasure and pain. Our first mistake is the belief that the circumstance gives the joy which we give to the circumstance. Life is an ecstasy. Life is sweet as nitrous oxide; and the fisherman dripping all day over a cold pond, the switchman at the railway intersection, the farmer in the field, the negro in the rice-swamp, the fop in the street, the hunter in the woods, the barrister with the jury, the belle at the ball, all ascribe a certain pleasure to their employment, which they themselves give it. Health and appetite impart the sweetness to sugar, bread, and meat. We fancy that our civilization has got on far, but we still come back to our primers.

We live by our imaginations, by our admirations, by our sentiments. The child walks amid heaps of illusions, which he does not like to have disturbed.

The boy, how sweet to him is his fancy! how dear the story of barons and battles! What a hero he is, whilst he feeds on his heroes! What a debt is his to imaginative books! He has no better friend or influence than Scott, Shakspeare, Plutarch, and Homer. The man lives to other objects, but who dare affirm that they are more real? Even the prose of the streets is full of refractions. In the life of the dreariest alderman, fancy enters into all details and colors them with rosy hue. He imitates the air and actions of people whom he admires, and is raised in his own eyes. He pays a debt quicker to a rich man than to a poor man. He wishes the bow and compliment of some leader in the state or in society; weighs what he says; perhaps he never comes nearer to him for that, but dies at last better contented for this amusement of his eyes and his fancy.

The world rolls, the din of life is never hushed. In London, in Paris, in Boston, in San Francisco, the carnival, the masquerade is at its height. Nobody drops his domino. The unities, the fictions of the piece it would be an impertinence to break. The chapter of fascinations is very long. Great is paint; nay, God is the painter; and we rightly accuse the critic who destroys too many illusions. Society does not love its unmaskers. It was wittily if somewhat bitterly said by D'Alembert, " *qu'un*

état de vapeur était un état très fâcheux, parce-
qu'il nous faisait voir les choses comme elles sont."
I find men victims of illusion in all parts of life.
Children, youths, adults and old men, all are led
by one bawble or another. Yoganidra, the goddess
of illusion, Proteus, or Momus, or Gylfi's Mocking,
— for the Power has many names, — is stronger
than the Titans, stronger than Apollo. Few have
overheard the gods or surprised their secret. Life
is a succession of lessons which must be lived to be
understood. All is riddle, and the key to a riddle
is another riddle. There are as many pillows of illusion as flakes in a snow-storm. We wake from
one dream into another dream. The toys to be
sure are various, and are graduated in refinement
to the quality of the dupe. The intellectual man
requires a fine bait; the sots are easily amused.
But everybody is drugged with his own frenzy, and
the pageant marches at all hours, with music and
banner and badge.

Amid the joyous troop who give in to the chari-
vari, comes now and then a sad-eyed boy whose
eyes lack the requisite refractions to clothe the
show in due glory, and who is afflicted with a tendency to trace home the glittering miscellany of
fruits and flowers to one root. Science is a search
after identity, and the scientific whim is lurking in
all corners. At the State Fair a friend of mine

complained that all the varieties of fancy pears in our orchards seem to have been selected by somebody who had a whim for a particular kind of pear, and only cultivated such as had that perfume; they were all alike. And I remember the quarrel of another youth with the confectioners, that when he racked his wit to choose the best comfits in the shops, in all the endless varieties of sweetmeat he could find only three flavors, or two. What then? Pears and cakes are good for something; and because you unluckily have an eye or nose too keen, why need you spoil the comfort which the rest of us find in them? I knew a humorist who in a good deal of rattle had a grain or two of sense. He shocked the company by maintaining that the attributes of God were two,— power and risibility, and that it was the duty of every pious man to keep up the comedy. And I have known gentlemen of great stake in the community, but whose sympathies were cold,— presidents of colleges and governors and senators, — who held themselves bound to sign every temperance pledge, and act with Bible societies and missions and peace-makers, and cry *Hist-a-boy!* to every good dog. We must not carry comity too far, but we all have kind impulses in this direction. When the boys come into my yard for leave to gather horse-chestnuts, I own I enter into Nature's game, and affect to grant the

permission reluctantly, fearing that any moment
they will find out the imposture of that showy chaff.
But this tenderness is quite unnecessary; the en-
chantments are laid on very thick. Their young
life is thatched with them. Bare and grim to tears
is the lot of the children in the hovel I saw yesterday; yet not the less they hung it round with frip-
pery romance, like the children of the happiest fortune, and talked of "the dear cottage where so
many joyful hours had flown." Well, this thatch-
ing of hovels is the custom of the country. Women,
more than all, are the element and kingdom of
illusion. Being fascinated, they fascinate. They
see through Claude-Lorraines. And how dare any
one, if he could, pluck away the *coulisses*, stage
effects and ceremonies, by which they live? Too
pathetic, too pitiable, is the region of affection, and
its atmosphere always liable to *mirage*.

We are not very much to blame for our bad
marriages. We live amid hallucinations; and this
especial trap is laid to trip up our feet with, and
all are tripped up first or last. But the mighty
Mother who had been so sly with us, as if she felt
that she owed us some indemnity, insinuates into
the Pandora-box of marriage some deep and serious
benefits and some great joys. We find a delight
in the beauty and happiness of children that makes
the heart too big for the body. In the worst-as-

sorted connections there is ever some mixture of true marriage. Teague and his jade get some just relations of mutual respect, kindly observation, and fostering of each other; learn something, and would carry themselves wiselier if they were now to begin.

'T is fine for us to point at one or another fine madman, as if there were any exempts. The scholar in his library is none. I, who have all my life heard any number of orations and debates, read poems and miscellaneous books, conversed with many geniuses, am still the victim of any new page; and if Marmaduke, or Hugh, or Moosehead, or any other, invent a new style or mythology, I fancy that the world will be all brave and right if dressed in these colors, which I had not thought of. Then at once I will daub with this new paint; but it will not stick. 'T is like the cement which the peddler sells at the door; he makes broken crockery hold with it, but you can never buy of him a bit of the cement which will make it hold when he is gone.

Men who make themselves felt in the world avail themselves of a certain fate in their constitution which they know how to use. But they never deeply interest us unless they lift a corner of the curtain, or betray, never so slightly, their penetration of what is behind it. 'T is the charm of practical men that outside of their practicality are a

certain poetry and play, as if they led the good
horse Power by the bridle, and preferred to walk,
though they can ride so fiercely. Bonaparte is intellectual, as well as Cæsar; and the best soldiers,
sea-captains and railway men have a gentleness
when off duty, a good-natured admission that there
are illusions, and who shall say that he is not their
sport? We stigmatize the cast-iron fellows who
cannot so detach themselves, as "dragon-ridden,"
"thunder-stricken," and fools of fate, with whatever powers endowed.

Since our tuition is through emblems and indi-
rections, it is well to know that there is method in
it, a fixed scale and rank above rank in the phan-
tasms. We begin low with coarse masks and rise
to the most subtle and beautiful. The red men
told Columbus "they had an herb which took away
fatigue;" but he found the illusion of "arriving
from the east at the Indies" more composing to
his lofty spirit than any tobacco. Is not our faith
in the impenetrability of matter more sedative than
narcotics? You play with jackstraws, balls, bowls,
horse and gun, estates and politics; but there are
finer games before you. Is not time a pretty toy?
Life will show you masks that are worth all your
carnivals. Yonder mountain must migrate into
your mind. The fine star-dust and nebulous blur
in Orion, "the portentous year of Mizar and Al-

cor," must come down and be dealt with in your household thought. What if you shall come to discern that the play and playground of all this pompous history are radiations from yourself, and that the sun borrows his beams? What terrible questions we are learning to ask! The former men believed in magic, by which temples, cities, and men were swallowed up, and all trace of them gone. We are coming on the secret of a magic which sweeps out of men's minds all vestige of theism and beliefs which they and their fathers held and were framed upon.

There are deceptions of the senses, deceptions of the passions, and the structural, beneficent illusions of sentiment and of the intellect. There is the illusion of love, which attributes to the beloved person all which that person shares with his or her family, sex, age, or condition, nay, with the human mind itself. 'T is these which the lover loves, and Anna Matilda gets the credit of them. As if one shut up always in a tower, with one window through which the face of heaven and earth could be seen, should fancy that all the marvels he beheld belonged to that window. There is the illusion of time, which is very deep; who has disposed of it? — or come to the conviction that what seems the *succession* of thought is only the distribution of wholes into causal series? The intellect sees that every atom carries the whole of Nature; that the mind opens to omnipotence; that, in the endless striving and ascents, the metamorphosis is entire, so that the soul doth not know itself in its own act when that act is perfected. There is illusion that shall deceive even the elect. There is illusion that shall deceive even the performer of the miracle. Though he make his body, he denies that he makes it. Though the world exist from thought, thought is daunted in presence of the world. One after the other we accept the mental laws, still resisting those which follow, which however must be accepted. But all our concessions only compel us to new profusion. And what avails it that science has come to treat space and time as simply forms of thought, and the material world as hypothetical, and withal our pretension of *property* and even of self-hood are fading with the rest, if, at last, even our thoughts are not finalities, but the incessant flowing and ascension reach these also, and each thought which yesterday was a finality, to-day is yielding to a larger generalization?

With such volatile elements to work in, 't is no wonder if our estimates are loose and floating. We must work and affirm, but we have no guess of the value of what we say or do. The cloud is now as big as your hand, and now it covers a county. That story of Thor, who was set to drain the drinking-horn in Asgard and to wrestle with the old woman and to run with the runner Lok, and presently found that he had been drinking up the sea, and wrestling with Time, and racing with Thought, — describes us, who are contending, amid these seeming trifles, with the supreme energies of Nature. We fancy we have fallen into bad company and squalid condition, low debts, shoe-bills, broken glass to pay for, pots to buy, butcher's meat, sugar, milk, and coal. ' Set me some great task, ye gods! and I will show my spirit.' ' Not so,' says the good Heaven ; ' plod and plough, vamp your old coats and hats, weave a shoestring ; great affairs and the best wine by and by.' Well, 'tis all phantasm ; and if we weave a yard of tape in all humility and as well as we can, long hereafter we shall see it was no cotton tape at all but some galaxy which we braided, and that the threads were Time and Nature.

We cannot write the order of the variable winds. How can we penetrate the law of our shifting moods and susceptibility ? Yet they differ as all and nothing. Instead of the firmament of yesterday, which our eyes require, it is to-day an egg-shell which coops us in ; we cannot even see what or where our stars of destiny are. From day to day the capital facts of human life are hidden from our eyes. Suddenly the mist rolls up and reveals them, and we think how much good time is gone that might have been saved had any hint of these things been shown. A sudden rise in the road shows us the system of mountains, and all the summits, which have been just as near us all the year, but quite out of mind. But these alternations are not without their order, and we are parties to our various fortune. If life seem a succession of dreams, yet poetic justice is done in dreams also. The visions of good men are good; it is the undisciplined will that is whipped with bad thoughts and bad fortunes. When we break the laws, we lose our hold on the central reality. Like sick men in hospitals, we change only from bed to bed, from one folly to another; and it cannot signify much what becomes of such castaways, wailing, stupid, comatose creatures, lifted from bed to bed, from the nothing of life to the nothing of death.

In this kingdom of illusions we grope eagerly for stays and foundations. There is none but a strict and faithful dealing at home and a severe barring out of all duplicity or illusion there. Whatever games are played with us, we must play no games with ourselves, but deal in our privacy with the last honesty and truth. I look upon the simple and childish virtues of veracity and honesty as the root of all that is sublime in character. Speak as you think, be what you are, pay your debts of all kinds.

I prefer to be owned as sound and solvent, and my word as good as my bond, and to be what cannot be skipped, or dissipated, or undermined, to all the *éclat* in the universe. This reality is the foundation of friendship, religion, poetry, and art. At the top or at the bottom of all illusions, I set the cheat which still leads us to work and live for appearances; in spite of our conviction, in all sane hours, that it is what we really are that avails, with friends, with strangers, and with fate or fortune.

One would think from the talk of men that riches and poverty were a great matter; and our civilization mainly respects it. But the Indians say that they do not think the white man, with his brow of care, always toiling, afraid of heat and cold, and keeping within doors, has any advantage of them. The permanent interest of every man is never to be in a false position, but to have the weight of Nature to back him in all that he does. Riches and poverty are a thick or thin costume; and our life — the life of all of us — identical. For we transcend the circumstance continually and taste the real quality of existence; as in our employments, which only differ in the manipulations but express the same laws; or in our thoughts, which wear no silks and taste no ice-creams. We see God face to face every hour, and know the savor of Nature.

The early Greek philosophers Heraclitus and Xenophanes measured their force on this problem of identity. Diogenes of Apollonia said that unless the atoms were made of one stuff, they could never blend and act with one another. But the Hindoos, in their sacred writings, express the liveliest feeling, both of the essential identity and of that illusion which they conceive variety to be. "The notions, '*I am*,' and '*This is mine*,' which influence mankind, are but delusions of the mother of the world. Dispel, O Lord of all creatures! the conceit of knowledge which proceeds from ignorance." And the beatitude of man they hold to lie in being freed from fascination.

The intellect is stimulated by the statement of truth in a trope, and the will by clothing the laws of life in illusions. But the unities of Truth and of Right are not broken by the disguise. There need never be any confusion in these. In a crowded life of many parts and performers, on a stage of nations, or in the obscurest hamlet in Maine or California, the same elements offer the same choices to each new comer, and, according to his election, he fixes his fortune in absolute Nature. It would be hard to put more mental and moral philosophy than the Persians have thrown into a sentence : —

"Fooled thou must be, though wisest of the wise :
Then be the fool of virtue, not of vice."

There is no chance and no anarchy in the universe. All is system and gradation. Every god is there sitting in his sphere. The young mortal enters the hall of the firmament; there is he alone with them alone, they pouring on him benedictions and gifts, and beckoning him up to their thrones. On the instant, and incessantly, fall snow-storms of illusions. He fancies himself in a vast crowd which sways this way and that and whose movement and doings he must obey: he fancies himself poor, orphaned, insignificant. The mad crowd drives hither and thither, now furiously commanding this thing to be done, now that. What is he that he should resist their will, and think or act for himself? Every moment new changes and new showers of deceptions to baffle and distract him. And when, by and by, for an instant, the air clears and the cloud lifts a little, there are the gods still sitting around him on their thrones, — they alone with him alone.